# THE C

## —C



Canadian chefs harvest
the best of farm and field

JANE HERMAN

Doubleday Canada Limited

CANADIAN CATALOGUING IN PUBLICATION DATA

Herman, Jane
The organic chef: Canadian chefs harvest the best of farm and field

Includes index.
ISBN 0-385-25408-3

1. Cookery (Natural foods). I. Title

TX741.H47 1993 641.5'637 C93-093065-7

Cover and text design by Tania Craan
Cover illustration by John Martin
Typeset by MacTrix DTP
Printed and bound in Canada
Printed on acid-free paper

Published in Canada by
Doubleday Canada Limited
105 Bond Street
Toronto, Ontario
M5B 1Y3

# Contents

## *Acknowledgements*

THANKS TO

My wonderful husband Rob, for his enduring patience and encouragement.

Meredith and Ted, with hope for the earth that you shall inherit.

Jamie Kennedy and Michael Stadtlander, two gifted chefs and great people, for giving me the opportunity to help realize their dream.

All the chefs and individuals who contributed material to this book.

Everyone who helped in ways large or small — Herb Barbolet, Don Blakney, David Cohlmeyer, Danielle Morin (*je vous remercie infiniment!*), Louise Moritsugu, Tomás Nimmo, Ken Peace, Melissa Philp, Dr. Sinclair Philip and Pat Shaver.

Jill Lambert of Doubleday, for her endless support and the vision that ultimately brought this project to fruition.

## *Introduction*

In the spring of 1989 I received a phone call from Jamie Kennedy, one of Canada's most renowned chefs, who sought my help in publicizing an event he was organizing with his good friend and colleague, Michael Stadtlander. As Kennedy put it, a group of restaurants were getting together late in the summer somewhere in the country to dramatize public awareness of the need for an organic farmers' market — a place where restaurateurs and chefs could obtain the freshest, cleanest products available directly from local producers, and mingle with one another on a weekly basis. I was intrigued that the initiative for this should come from a chef.

A so-called "gastronomic walking tour," the first annual Feast of Fields, held in September 1989, was essentially the ultimate picnic for food and wine lovers who wandered through vineyards and fields, sampling the delights of more than thirty participating restaurants, wineries and breweries at various intervals.

The proceeds from the Feast of Fields were used to establish Knives and Forks, an organization whose initial members were chefs who sought to establish closer ties with local producers. Six months later, the Knives and Forks Market, a small farmers' market comprised exclusively of vendors selling organic foods, opened in Toronto. I remained actively involved with Knives and Forks until May of 1992, when I began working on this book. During those three years, my awareness of where our food comes from and how it is grown increased dramatically. I felt that a cookbook that linked recipes to the origins of their ingredients might have a positive impact on the public's understanding of the environmental consequences of conventional agriculture, as well as open the consumer's eye to the superior flavour and quality of organically-grown produce.

These recipes, which I collected during the summer and fall of 1992, represent the effort of chefs from nearly every region of the country to use seasonal, local and organically-grown ingredients as the basis for cuisine. This is not a definitive edition but rather a representative sampling of Canadian chefs who favour the use of organic, seasonal and locally-grown ingredients wherever possible. These recipes clearly demonstrate the vast range of ingredients we have to work with, and the breadth of talent we have cooking in this country today.

"Although we live in a time when everything is available to us year-round it is always best to first examine what is available locally," says Jamie Kennedy. Cuisine, or cooking style, is traditionally based upon the plants, animals, weather, soil and history that are indiginous to an area. Working with ingredients that are obtained locally put us in closer touch with our native bioregion, and encourages economic self-sufficiency and the development of a unique food style. Furthermore, foods always taste best right at their source. Foods that are shipped great distances generally have had most of the flavour bred out of them and are also treated with chemicals that delay their ripening.

Seasonality is another concept that has virtually disappeared in this era of the "global table." Until quite recently, life flowed according to the seasons, and the appearance of foods that marked each changing season was greatly anticipated. Traditionally foods were only enjoyed at the peak of flavour, or naturally preserved, either by canning or drying, for later use. Because so much is now available to us from every corner of the world, it is more difficult than ever before to remain true to our natural traditions. However, one should still begin with the seasons. Once you have tasted tomatoes at their peak of flavour you realize how inferior they are at every other time of the year. With this understanding, you will be able to give proper attention to what is best at each time of year. Although it often means delaying gratification, we need to redevelop a sense of discrimination about what we are eating and when. Only then can we savour the true pleasure of foods in their appropriate seasons.

### *What Is Organic Food?*

The 1977 edition of *The Groaning Board Cookbook* contains a recipe for "Organic Pizza" which typifies the misconceptions about organic food that still persist today: "In actual fact," writes author Harry Stinson, "there's not really much 'organic' about this pizza. True, we use a wholewheat pita bun as the base, and a considerably more interesting collection of toppings, but it seems that *people will believe that anything is organic as long as somewhere within, or upon, there be a bean sprout.*" [my ital.] When I asked people at random in Toronto's St. Lawrence Market, "What is organic food?" the answers ranged from "things that are not sprayed" to "healthy food," to "health foods, you know, granola or tofu," to "vegetarian food."

There remains a good deal of confusion, that often borders on outright suspicion, surrounding the use of the word organic, when referring to food. A number of the chefs whose recipes appear in this book have, at one time or another, been reluctant to indicate that certain items on their menus contain organically-grown ingredients, for fear of those items being perceived as "health food." "The organic industry has had a major impact on agriculture," says Tomás Nimmo, of Organic Farm Services, a leading consultant in the organic field. "But organics has not yet been accepted by the mainstream."

"The very mention of the 'O word' makes farmers uneasy," says Ted Zettel, who is president of the Ecological Farmers Association of Ontario, an organization that helps farmers gain the basic knowledge needed to adopt ecologically sound management practices. "There has been a lot of negative publicity surrounding the use of the word organic," he says. "We shouldn't be concentrating our efforts on whether or not there are residues in conventionally-grown foods," he says, "but on the effect our farming practices are having on the environment."

In technical terms, organic food is food that has been grown according to a system of ecological soil management that respects the balance of nature. The soil is continually replenished by the addition and preservation of organic matter, or humus, which is accomplished through such activities as crop rotation, the addition of manure, composting and mulching and the addition of balanced mineral supplements, chosen from a list of acceptable substances.

Organic gardeners and farmers treat the soil as a living system whose nutrients contain the substances needed to encourage plant growth while simultaneously suppressing the development of plant diseases. Human and environmental health is of primary importance and the application of any substances that may pose potential risks are strictly prohibited. The organic system provides optimum conditions for soil biological activity. Just as a person who is fed a proper, balanced diet will be healthier and full of life, so plants grown in a healthy soil environment will also thrive. Under such conditions, and, using pest-resistant varieties of nutrients, insect, disease and weed problems are kept to a minimum.

In order to commercially market foods as organically grown, farmers must be able to document, through the generation of an audit trail, that they have complied with an extensive set of standards that cover all aspects of farm management. This record permits tracing to the wholesaler, retailer or consumer the sources and amounts of all inputs and all steps between harvest and sale. These standards cover all aspects of food production, from wild rice and maple syrup production, to animal husbandry, milling and fruit and vegetable processing, to the handling of crops after harvest. Farms are inspected every year by a group of individuals representing one of several certification agencies.

To be sure that the food you are buying is in fact organic, check that it has been certified by a reputable international certification agency, such as O.C.I.A. (Organic Crop Improvement Association), or Demeter, also known as the Society for Biodynamic Farming and Gardening. O.C.I.A.-certified farms are provided with small stickers for such purposes. Some of the practices may vary slightly from group to group, but only certification assures you of the quality of the food you are buying.

The present system of food distribution has created an agricultural system that has caused widespread environmental degradation, including extensive water pollution from herbicides, pesticides and chemical fertilizers, large scale loss of topsoil and soil erosion. Water pollution is probably the most damaging and widespread environmental effect of agricultural production. Half of all polluted U.S. rivers and lakes are polluted by agricultural chemicals and between 450 and 500 million pounds of pesticides are applied in the U.S. each year.* Pesticides have been detected in the groundwater of twenty-six states as a result of normal agricultural practices. Although pesticides have kept pest damage to a minimum, pesticide-resistant species of many insects commonly develop, requiring increased applications of a stronger concentration.

Because the consumption of meat and animal protein is so firmly entrenched in our culture, millions of acres of land have been unnecessarily cleared for cattle grazing. The runoff from animal wastes is an additional, major contributor to water pollution, and millions of pounds of grain are fed to cattle while people all around the world go hungry. I won't explore the rather inhumane conditions under which most animals are raised, or the health and environmental impact of consuming animal protein; rather I suggest you read John Robbins' *Diet for a New America*, an excellent, eye-opening book on this subject.

Few of us realize the impact that our food choices have on our own health and on the health of the environment. Today's consumers are inundated by a variety of forces that subtly as well as overtly influence what we eat. Large-scale agricultural policy does not advocate organic farming, and chemical companies spend millions of dollars annually lobbying federal and provincial governments, while the organic industry has no such spokespeople. Agricultural marketing boards, large supermarket chains, trans-national corporations and food processing and distributing conglomerates are all interconnected to ensure the consumption of mass-produced varieties of certain crops, like potatoes, which promote the existence of monoculture (the over-cultivation of a single crop variety.)

Despite the consumer's desire for cleaner food, a number of factors are currently impeding the industry's efforts to make inroads in the marketplace. "Consumer expectations concerning visual quality and appearance of produce are exceptionally high," says Pat Shaver, horticultural crop advisor with the Ontario Ministry of Agriculture. If you have ever watched consumers selecting produce in a supermarket you have probably noticed that it is appearance rather than flavour that determines what we buy. While working picking apples in New Zealand one summer, Shaver was horrified to discover that, "Fifty percent of the apples were discarded because of inappropriate visual quality — most were bumpy or irregular in some way." Only education can overcome our expectations of perfect-looking produce — which sadly is most often achieved through inordinate amounts of chemicals. Ironically, many varieties of organically-grown produce often look far better than that grown commercially, but never reach the average consumer.

And then there is the cost factor. While locally-grown organic produce sold in season at farmers' markets may cost even less than that purchased at the local supermarket, organically-grown food can cost anywhere from ten to forty percent more than that generally available. This is because organic food is grown on a much smaller scale, with no economic distribution system to serve it, using labour-intensive production methods. Overall demand is still relatively low, and post-production standards require special, often costly methods of handling. Coupled with cost is the lack of wide availability: one must often go out of one's way to purchase organically-grown foods, and this inconvenience is a major deterrent to the consumer.

The availability of organically-grown foods will only increase in response to increased demand for them. That is why all of us who know and appreciate the difference must begin by taking the initiative to purchase organically-grown foods whenever and wherever they are available.

As I write, a number of exciting changes are occurring in the Canadian organic industry, whose impact will be seen in the years to come. In 1992, The Canadian Organic Unity Project established minimum standards for organic certification and accreditation throughout Canada. Various organizations and experts from all regions of the country provided input into the legislation, which will ensure consistency throughout the industry and the country and boost consumer confidence. National standards will give a better indication of just how many acres in the country are being cultivated organically; will facilitate the import and export of organic food (Canadian standards, for example, are higher than those in the U.S.); and will be a great benefit to those who must consume organic foods for medical reasons.

In Ontario, a coalition of twenty-eight conventional agricultural groups recently released its "Environmental Farm Agenda," so farmers could identify the key environmental issues facing Ontario agriculture. Participating farms will now, with government support, be able to identify areas of potential environmental risk on their farms, and set realistic goals to minimize those risks. Increasingly, the organics industry is beginning to have a major impact on agriculture, having forced changes at other levels. These are positive steps, but they are only the beginning. As consumers we have the opportunity to make a positive impact on the environment every day just by the kinds of foods put on our table.

It is no longer a secret that organically-grown food tastes far superior to anything that is grown commercially. What I hope you will discover in these pages is how choosing foods that have been organically grown can also have a tremendous impact on the health of our environment. The recipes contained in this book prove that a cuisine based on local, seasonal and organically-grown ingredients is not only healthful, but can be delicious and exciting as well. These recipes are a point of departure to help you discover the potential in that which can be found all around us.

---

* National Research Council, *Alternative Agriculture*, Committee on the Role of Alternative Farming Methods in Modern Production Agriculture, National Academy Press, Washington, D.C., 1989. (The book is based on U.S. agriculture, but similar problems will be found in Canada).

# BREADS

*Newly incorporated in May of 1992, Ecco Il Pane is the first bakery of its kind on the Vancouver food scene to offer artisan Italian and country breads. A stone hearth and a steam-injection method produces Ecco's signature crackled-crisp crust, while aged starters, slow rise and intense heat give the authentic hand-shaped loaves a full-bodied flavour and moistness. All flours are fresh-milled in the bakery itself from organically grown grains, and no sugar or dairy products are ever used. Ecco's breads are distributed in grocery stores, health food stores and specialty shops, as well as being sold in the Granville Island Market.*

*Ecco was conceived by Christopher Brown, a chef who worked with Umberto Menghi for seven years and who always had a passion for breads. Recognizing that there was a need for the rustic breads he wanted to produce, Brown went on to create a line that consists of a dozen sweet and savoury breads, including Pane alle Olive, Roasted Tomato–Garlic and Fig–Walnut, as well as his signature Tuscan, Vancouver's favourite restaurant bread.*

*Because flour milled from organically ground grain must be handled and processed somewhat differently from what is produced commercially, it is not always available, notes Pamela Gaudreault, Brown's partner and Ecco's business manager. Gaudreault is hopeful that over the next few years as consumers become aware of the superior results that organically-grown ingredients produce, as well as the environmental implications of supporting the conventional system, that fresh-milled, organically-grown flour will become more available. In the meantime, the bakery buys its grain from organic farmers and grinds it into flour with its own mill. Using freshly ground flour enhances the flavour, texture and authenticity of the product, says Gaudreault.*

*The biggest adjustment in establishing the business, Gaudreault found, was the change in working hours. Ecco Il Pane bakes all night — from 12:00 p.m. to 8:00 a.m. — so that the city can enjoy its wonderful creations like Dolce Imio, a sweet Italian bread with currants and marsala wine, throughout the day. "But," she adds, "knowing how much people enjoy and appreciate the products keeps you going."*

# Mixed Grain Bread with Leeks

CHRISTOPHER BROWN
Ecco Il Pane Bakery Inc.
*Vancouver, British Columbia*

MAKES 2 LOAVES

| | | |
|---|---|---|
| 1 pkg | dry yeast | 1 pkg |
| ¼ cup | water | 50 mL |
| 1 tsp | honey | 5 mL |
| 1½ cups | water | 375 mL |
| 2¼ cups | unbleached all purpose flour | 550 mL |
| ¾ cup | Nunweiler's dark rye flour | 175 mL |
| ½ cup | organic corn meal | 125 mL |
| 1½ cups | organic whole wheat flour | 375 mL |
| 1 tsp | sea salt | 5 mL |
| 1¾ cups | organic walnuts (toasted) | 425 mL |
| 2 | medium leeks | 2 |
| 1½ Tbsp | olive oil | 20 mL |

• Clean leeks and cut into ¾-inch/2-cm pieces. Sauté in olive oil on low heat for 5 minutes until wilted and lightly browned on edges. Let cool completely.

• In a small bowl combine the yeast, the ¼ cup/50 mL of water, and honey and let stand for 10 minutes or until the yeast is foamy.

• Place remaining 1½ cups/375 mL water in a mixing bowl. Add the yeast mixture. Using a wooden spoon or the paddle of an electric mixer, slowly add enough of the combined flours, corn meal and salt until the mixture is too thick to work with the spoon or until the dough gathers on the paddle. Set aside the remaining flour mixture.

• Turn dough onto a floured surface or attach the dough hook. Knead in walnuts and leeks. Add remaining flour, if necessary, and knead 5–10 minutes by hand (3–5 minutes by machine) to obtain a springy, non-sticky dough. Place in an oiled bowl and let rise until double (45 minutes to 1 hour).

• Shape into loaves. Sprinkle corn meal on a baking stone or cookie sheet lined with parchment paper. Bake at 375–400°F/190–200°C for approximately 35 minutes or until bread sounds hollow when tapped on the bottom.

Most organic flours and dry ingredients can be obtained through Horizon Distributors, Burnaby, B.C. (*See Source Information at back of book.*)

*Located in the scenic foothills of the Rocky Mountains, The Robin's Nest Bed and Breakfast is an organic farm that has been the Jackson family homestead since 1896. Renowned for their wholesome, nutritious food and gracious hospitality, Dorothy and Bill Jackson offer guests a taste of a way of life that is becoming less and less common. Mrs. Jackson personally bakes all of the breads, buns, muffins and biscuits that she serves to her guests from freshly milled organic grains. Her baked goods are accompanied by an array of home-made preserves, made with berries including saskatoon, from her own orchard, and in spring, dandelion jelly. Rainbow trout is caught from their own farm pond, poached and served with fresh herbs, mushrooms, tomatoes and other seasonal vegetables from the garden. The four or more course breakfast includes an abundance of local fresh fruit and yogurt. As the autumn air becomes cool and crisp, baked stuffed apples, cranberry-glazed pears and home-made whole grain cereals find their way onto the breakfast table.*

*The saskatoon berry, which once grew wild in great abundance on the prairies, is an important part of the area's heritage. Similar to a wild blueberry, but perhaps a bit smaller and more purple, with a distinctive, tart taste, the berries were harvested by native people, who dried and pounded them for winter use. Mrs. Jackson recalls with great fondness how in her early days in Alberta, it was a great tradition to pick the saskatoons every July. "Your mom would can them, maybe adding a little rhubarb to give them a little juice, and you would eat them all winter." Now that so much land has been cleared, most of the wild berries are gone, but a new industry is developing to take cuttings of the vanishing wild species and domesticate them. The Jacksons, in fact, have their own saskatoon orchard on their farm. The domestic berries are a little more fleshy than the wild berries, says Mrs. Jackson, and not as seedy.*

*"I wouldn't think of using anything but organic flour, vegetables from the garden, home-grown berries, when I cook," says Mrs. Jackson. "We're a modern family, but some of the old-fashioned ways are still the best."*

# Oat Bran Muffins with Saskatoon Berries

DOROTHY JACKSON
The Robin's Nest Bed and Breakfast
*Calgary, Alberta*

MAKES 12 MEDIUM-SIZED MUFFINS

| | | |
|---|---|---|
| 1 | egg, lightly beaten | 1 |
| ½ cup | milk or yogurt | 125 mL |
| ¼ cup | vegetable oil | 50 mL |
| ¼ cup | honey | 50 mL |
| ⅔ cup | applesauce | 150 mL |
| 1 tsp | vanilla | 5 mL |
| 1 cup | whole wheat flour | 250 mL |
| 1 tsp | baking powder | 5 mL |
| 1 tsp | baking soda | 5 mL |
| 1 cup | oat bran | 250 mL |
| 1 cup | saskatoon berries | 250 mL |

- Combine egg, milk, oil, honey, applesauce and vanilla in a blender container or in the bowl of a food processor and mix. Transfer to a large bowl.
- In another bowl mix flour, baking powder, baking soda and oat bran. Add saskatoons.
- Stir into egg mixture until only just combined. Pour into greased or paper-lined muffin tins and bake 15 minutes in a 375°/190°C oven.

*"Organics makes sense in a lot of ways," says Harry Beck, of Beck's Bakery, in Pembroke, Ontario, "nutritionally, economically, and environmentally."*

*On his own Demeter-certified farm Beck grows grains that he grinds into flour himself. "Organic flours contain the whole germ of the wheat, and therefore, can turn rancid quickly. Conventional processing treats the flour to inhibit spoilage, but, Beck emphasizes, "the best results are achieved by grinding the flour fresh ourselves."*

# Onion Herb Bread

HARRY BECK
Beck's Bakery
*Pembroke, Ontario*

MAKES 2 LOAVES

| | | |
|---|---|---|
| 2 pkgs | dry yeast | 2 pkgs |
| 2½ cups + 2 Tbsp | cool water | 650 mL |
| 8 cups | whole wheat flour | 1 kg |
| 2 Tbsp | diced onions | 25 mL |
| 2 Tbsp | fresh dill, chopped | 25 mL |
| 1 Tbsp | fresh parsley, chopped | 15 mL |
| 1 tsp | fresh thyme (leaves only), chopped | 5 mL |
| 1 Tbsp | sea salt | 15 mL |
| 6 Tbsp | ground nuts or bran | 100 mL |

• Dissolve the yeast in the water. In another bowl combine the whole wheat flour, diced onions, dill, parsley, thyme and sea salt. Add the water/yeast mixture and knead vigorously for about 20 minutes or until the dough no longer sticks to the bowl.

• Allow to rest 40–60 minutes until the batch has doubled in size.

• Knead again for 5–10 minutes, and divide into 3 equal-sized loaves. Place in greased bread pans. Moisten the top by brushing or spraying with the water and sprinkle with ground nuts or bran.

• Allow loaves to rise for 10–20 minutes. Preheat oven to 400°F/200°C and bake for approximately 45 minutes.

*One of the oldest known grains, spelt was grown in Europe 9,000 years ago and was also mentioned in the Old Testament. Ecologically, it is considered the ideal grain, for it requires a minimum of care and can grow in any climate.*

*The spelt kernel is tightly enclosed in a strong, hard hull that protects it from air pollutants and many diseases that commonly afflict other grains. This hull must be removed before milling for consumption. Unlike wheat, whose bran and germ bud are removed during milling, the vital substances in the inner kernel of spelt cannot be milled away.*

*One of the most nutritious of all grains, spelt contains the essential amino acids, and is high in vitamin B and the complex carbohydrates. Highly water soluble, the nutrients in spelt can be readily absorbed by the body with a minimum of digestive work. Bread made from spelt flour is finely textured and satisfying, and can truly be called "the staff of life."*

*When Uta Nagel arrived in Canada from Germany in 1983, she bemoaned the lack of hearty, rich-textured bread that she had been accustomed to in her homeland. Shortly afterward, the industrious young woman rented a stall at the weekly St. Lawrence Market, baked all day Thursday and Friday, and arrived at the crack of dawn each Saturday morning laden with her distinctive, lavishly braided whole-grain breads and huge muffins. Concerned about personal health, Nagel went out of her way to obtain organic flour, which she uses exclusively. To develop their unique texture, she kneads all of her breads by hand, a practice she maintains in her factory operation today.*

*Today, Grainfields is a successful commercial bakery, with two retail outlets, and wholesale distribution to restaurants and health food stores across Ontario.*

# Spelt Poppyseed Twist

UTA NAGEL
Grainfields Bakery Ltd.
*Toronto, Ontario*

MAKES 1 LOAF

| | | |
|---|---|---|
| 3 cups | organic spelt flour | 750 mL |
| ½ cup | poppy seeds | 125 mL |
| 1 Tbsp | instant yeast | 15 mL |
| 1 tsp | sea salt | 5 mL |
| ¾ cup | sourdough sponge (see pages 12–13) | 150 mL |
| 2 cups | water | 500 mL |

- Mix all dry ingredients together in a large bowl. Then add the sourdough and water. Mix together to form a soft dough.
- Turn dough out onto a lightly floured kneading surface and knead gently until smooth (about 10 minutes). Wash, dry and lightly oil the mixing bowl. Return dough to bowl, cover with a cloth, and let rest in a warm place for 1 hour or until doubled in bulk.
- Divide dough into 2 equal parts and roll into 12-inch/30-cm strands. Cut each strand in half again to make 4 pieces. Roll each piece into 12-inch/30-cm lengths. Twist or braid all 4 pieces together and let rise again for 30 minutes.
- Bake at 375°F/190°C for 40 minutes.

Boker Organic Farms in Elmvale, Ontario, sell their spelt flour at the Barrie Farmers' Market, Barrie City Hall. They also sell it at their farm. (*See Source Information at back of book.*)

# Whole Wheat Yogurt Bread with Fresh Herbs and Cumin

UTA NAGEL
Grainfields Bakery Ltd.
*Toronto, Ontario*

MAKES 2 LOAVES

| | | |
|---|---|---|
| 1½ Tbsp | instant (powdered) yeast | 20 mL |
| 2 Tbsp | sourdough sponge (recipe follows) | 25 mL |
| 1 cup | warm water | 250 mL |
| 3 cups | hard organic whole wheat flour | 750 mL |
| 1 cup | hard organic unbleached white flour | 250 mL |
| 2 cups | organic light rye flour | 500 mL |
| 2 tsp | sea salt | 10 mL |
| 1¾ cups | water | 425 mL |
| 1 cup | yogurt | 250 mL |
| 1 Tbsp | fresh basil, chopped | 15 mL |
| 1 Tbsp | rosemary, chopped | 15 mL |
| 1 Tbsp | fresh thyme, chopped | 15 mL |
| 1 Tbsp | cumin | 15 mL |

***Sourdough Sponge***

| | | |
|---|---|---|
| 3½ cups | stone ground rye flour | 875 mL |
| 1 cup | water | 250 mL |
| ¼ cup | buttermilk | 50 mL |

- In a small bowl, mix together the instant yeast, sourdough sponge, and water. Let stand until bubbly (about 5–10 minutes).
- In a large bowl, mix well the flours, sea salt, water and yogurt, in that order. Make a well in the centre and pour in the yeast mixture.

• Add herbs to dough and mix thoroughly. You should have a soft dough.
• Turn dough out onto a lightly floured kneading surface and gently knead for 10 minutes. Wash and dry the mixing bowl, oil lightly, and return the bread, covering with a cloth, for 1 hour or until doubled in bulk.
• Turn dough out onto kneading surface. Cut in half, shape into 2 loaves, and place in 2 greased loaf pans.
• Bake at 375°F/190°C for 40–50 minutes.

### *Sourdough Sponge*

• Combine in a stoneware bowl or porcelain container:

| | | |
|---|---|---|
| 1 cup | rye flour, at room temperature | 250 mL |
| ⅓ cup | warm water | 75 mL |
| ¼ cup | warm buttermilk | 50 mL |

• Cover with a cloth and let sit in a warm draft-free place for 24 hours. Stir and let set for another 24 hours.
• Mix together with the above:

| | | |
|---|---|---|
| 2½ cups | rye flour | 625 mL |
| ⅔ cup | water | 150 mL |

Let sit another 24 hours. The sourdough sponge is now ready. Any leftover sponge should be refrigerated. It will remain fresh for 1–2 weeks.

*Wild rice is the seed of a native North American grass, and was once a staple food for the Ojibway Indians. It is similar in appearance to domesticated paddy rice, a hybrid that was developed in the laboratories of agricultural schools, which is often mistakenly marketed as wild rice. True wild rice is usually harvested by shattering the grains from the plant stalks by mechanical means, whereas paddy rice is cut with combines to separate it from its stalk. After being harvested, wild rice is fermented in piles and then heated to develop its flavour and facilitate hulling.*

*Kagiwiosa Manomin harvests, processes and markets O.C.I.A.-certified wild rice using traditional practices. In order to qualify for certification, harvest areas must be free of prohibited materials for a minimum of five years prior to harvest, and potential contamination is monitored each year that certification is renewed.*

# Wild Rice Bread

RUTH McCASLIN
Kagiwiosa Manomin Inc.
*Dinorwic, Ontario*

MAKES 2 LOAVES OR 24 ROLLS

| | | |
|---|---|---|
| ½ cup | wild rice | 125 mL |
| 3 cups | water | 750 mL |
| 1 tsp | cooking oil | 5 mL |
| ¼ cup | cold pressed oil, such as sunflower | 50 mL |
| 2 Tbsp | yeast | 25 mL |
| ½ cup | warm water | 125 mL |
| ¼ cup | molasses | 50 mL |
| 2 cups | warm water | 500 mL |
| ½ tsp | ginger | 2 mL |
| 2 tsp | salt | 10 mL |
| 2 cups | whole wheat flour | 500 mL |

| | | |
|---|---|---|
| ½ cup | wheat bran | 125 mL |
| ½ cup | oat bran | 125 mL |
| 5–6 cups | unbleached white flour | 1.25–1.5 L |
| 1 | egg beaten with 1 Tbsp/15 mL water | 1 |

• In a saucepan combine the wild rice, 3 cups/750 mL water, and the 1 tsp/5 mL oil. Bring to a boil and simmer, uncovered, for 30 minutes until the rice is tender. Put the rice and the cooking liquid in a large mixing bowl.

• In a small bowl combine the yeast, ½ cup/125 mL warm water, and the molasses. Stir and set aside until the yeast bubbles, then add to the rice, along with the remaining water, both oils, ginger, salt, whole wheat flour, wheat bran, oat bran and 5 cups/1.25 L of the unbleached white flour. Beat the dough with a heavy spoon or dough hook until the texture is smooth. Gradually add as much of the remaining unbleached white flour as necessary to make a smooth, unsticky dough.

• Butter or oil a clean mixing bowl and place the dough in it, turning it to oil the surface. Let rise in a warm place for 1½ hours until doubled in bulk.

• Punch the dough down and turn out onto a lightly floured surface. Shape into 2 loaves or 24 rolls and place in two greased bread pans or baking sheets. Cover with a towel and let rise another 30–40 minutes.

• Preheat oven to 350°F/180°C. Brush the loaves with the egg mixture and sprinkle with sesame seeds or sliced almonds if desired. Bake for 1 hour until golden brown. (Rolls only need 30–35 minutes of baking).

# Whole Wheat Focaccia with Asiago and Herbs

CHRISTOPHER BROWN
Ecco Il Pane Bakery Inc.
*Vancouver, British Columbia*

MAKES 1 LARGE LOAF

| | | |
|---|---|---|
| 1 Tbsp + 2 tsp | dry yeast | 20 mL |
| 1⅔ cups | warm water | 400 mL |
| 1 Tbsp | honey | 15 mL |
| 2 Tbsp | extra-virgin olive oil | 25 mL |
| ⅓ cup | water | 75 mL |
| 3¼ cups | unbleached all purpose flour | 800 mL |
| 1¾ cups | organic whole wheat flour | 425 mL |
| 1 Tbsp | salt | 15 mL |
| ½ cup | grated asiago cheese | 125 mL |
| ¼ cup | coarsely chopped fresh herbs | 50 mL |

- Combine yeast, water and honey and let stand for 10 minutes in a mixing bowl. Add olive oil and remaining water.
- Using the paddle or whisk of an electric mixer, add the flours and salt to the liquid mixture at medium speed.
- Add the asiago and fresh herbs and combine well. The consistency should resemble a cake batter. Pour into a well-oiled 9 x 13-inch/23 x 33-cm cake pan and smooth out. Sprinkle with olive oil and spread the oil over the surface.
- Let rise until doubled. Bake at 425°F/220°C for 25 minutes or until golden brown on the surface. Cool for 10 minutes in the pan and then turn out onto a cake rack to cool completely. Cut into desired portions and serve.

Some of the flours and dry goods may be obtained from Horizon Distributors in Burnaby, B.C. Ecco Il Pane obtains its fresh herbs from Glorious Garnishes. (*See Source Information at back of book.*)

# SOUPS

*"Cheddar is the flavour of our country," says Daniel Lapointe, who has been making raw milk cheeses on his organic farm in Quebec's Eastern Townships since 1986. Personal health and the environment figure prominently in every aspect of the farm's operation, from the way the dairy herd is managed, through the cheesemaking process, to the materials used in packaging the final product. "Our goal is zero pollution," he emphasizes.*

*Cows graze on sweet, unsprayed pastures, 1,400 feet above sea level, and are fed organic grains during the winter. Alternative medicines are administered only if the need arises. Special soaps and cleaning systems maintain an extremely high level of cleanliness among the herd.*

*To achieve the superior flavor and texture that characterize his cheeses, Lapointe, who oversees the only certified organic cheesemaking operation in Canada, begins with raw (unpasteurized) whole milk. The milk is then warmed very gently (a temperature of 98°F/37°C is maintained throughout the warming process). This makes the fat molecules, which are naturally present in the milk, more digestible. And because the milk is never overheated, the texture of the proteins is not broken down. This gives Lapointe's cheeses their distinctive richness.*

*Commercial cheesemakers, by comparison, start with homogenized and often lowfat milk. Enzymes such as rennet or pepsin are then added to the milk. The mixture is heated, often to temperatures as high as 160°F/72°C. This actually has the reverse effect on the digestive system than is intended: the enzyme adheres to the fat molcules, thus increasing the rate of absorption of fat in the digestive system. (The fat content of the organic cheese is higher to start with, but less of it is absorbed in the digestive system due to the way the milk is handled.)*

*Lapointe's cheese is packaged in paraffin, not vacuum sealed in plastic, for several reasons. Like the cork on a bottle of wine, the paraffin enables the gases to escape as the cheese ages, while it prevents air from entering. And the paraffin is reusable — it can be made into candles. Lastly, the paraffin is covered with a piece of cellophane (a natural product, made from wood, which can ultimately be broken down naturally).*

*Lapointe's cheese has a long shelf life — if rewrapped in the paraffin, it will keep for five to seven years in the refrigerator. When was the last time a piece of commercially produced cheese remained fresh for that long at your house?*

*If Delapointe cheeses are not available in your area, Daniel Lapointe will ship them to you directly. Once you experience the taste and texture of Lapointe's cheeses you will never want to settle for anything less.* (See Source Information at back of book.)

# Cheddar Cheese Soup with Wild Leeks

KEVIN SNOOK
The Thirsty Fox
*Grand Bend, Ontario*

SERVES 6

| | | |
|---|---|---|
| 6 cups | chicken stock | 1.5 L |
| 1 Tbsp | cognac | 15 mL |
| pinch | paprika | pinch |
| 1 tsp | worcestershire sauce | 5 mL |
| pinch | nutmeg | pinch |
| ¼ cup | unsalted butter | 50 mL |
| ½ cup | wild leeks, white part only, washed, trimmed and finely sliced (save the greens for garnish) | 125 mL |
| ¼ cup | all purpose flour | 50 mL |
| 1 cup | whipping cream | 250 mL |
| 1 lb | aged white cheddar cheese, grated | 454 g |
| ½ tsp | salt | 2 mL |
| ½ tsp | white pepper | 2 mL |

• Bring the chicken stock to a gentle boil, then add the cognac, paprika, worcestershire and nutmeg. Set stock aside until it has cooled slightly.
• Meanwhile, melt the butter over medium heat in a thick-bottomed saucepan, add the leeks, and sauté over low heat until soft and translucent. Add flour a little at a time, stirring with a wooden spoon. Cook for 5 minutes.
• Slowly whisk in the stock, stirring constantly. Return to a medium-low heat and simmer for 20 minutes. Stir in whipping cream and reheat, but do not boil, then remove from heat.
• Add cheese gradually, stirring constantly until smooth. Season with salt and pepper, strain, and serve.
• Garnish with sliced blanched green of the wild leeks.

Wild leeks are available in season from Cookstown Greens. Canada's only certified organic cheddar cheese is produced by Daniel Lapointe, Ferme Delapointe, Bury, Quebec. (*See Source Information at back of book.*)

*The Okanagan Valley is to British Columbia what Sonoma county is to California. This productive, fertile region is known for its high-quality berries and tree fruits. Because the dry climate helps to minimize many diseases that commonly affect vinifera, a local wine industry is also developing.*

*Cedar Creek Wines, whose dry table wines are a favourite of chef John Rogers, is a local estate winery in the Okanagan Valley. Although they are not certified organic, winemaker Ann Sperling notes that because of the climate they rarely need to apply any pesticides or fungicides, and have not used any chemical fertilizers in the eight years they have been producing. (For more on chef Rogers, see page 120.)*

# Chilled Okanagan Peach Soup

JOHN ROGERS
Windows on the Bay, Coast Plaza Hotel
*Vancouver, British Columbia*

SERVES 4

| | | |
|---|---|---|
| 1 lb | large, fresh Okanagan peaches | 454 g |
| 1 Tbsp | finely chopped strong white onions | 15 mL |
| 1 tsp | grated fresh ginger | 5 mL |
| 1 Tbsp | unsalted butter | 15 mL |
| 1 Tbsp | granulated sugar | 15 mL |
| ½ tsp | ground coriander | 2 mL |
| ¼ cup | white wine (pinot blanc from Cedar Creek) | 50 mL |
| 2 cups | fresh chicken stock | 500 mL |
| ½ cup | sour cream | 125 mL |
| ¼ cup | low fat yogurt | 50 mL |
| | fresh mint sprigs, for garnish | |

• Dice peaches, removing stone. (Do not peel.) Sauté peaches, onions and grated ginger in the butter. Add sugar, ground coriander and white wine. Bring to a boil.
• Add warm chicken stock and boil for 10–15 minutes. Blend in a food processor until smooth. Cool. Season if desired.
• Fold in sour cream. Serve topped with a little low fat natural yogurt and a sprig of fresh mint.

The restaurant obtains peaches from Glorious Garnishes. They are also sold at the Granville Island Market. Windows on the Bay uses a lot of Cedar Creek Wines, which are distributed by Grady Wines. (*See Source Information at back of book.*)

*Martin's Catering handles all kinds of private and corporate functions, no matter how large or small, and incorporates organic ingredients whenever possible. Contracts have included a romantic dinner for two in a limousine, food for 5,000 at a frisbee tournament in Sunnybrook Park, and a film shoot in Latvia during the summer of 1992 (Martin Ritins, the owner, was one of two North American caterers contacted who could speak Latvian.)*

*Chef Alli Millar of Martin's Catering originally began to use organic ingredients because of the unusual varieties that were available from organic farmers. Now, she says, it is the flavour of the vegetables, the tenderness of the meat, and the knowledge that her choice is benefitting the health of the land that continue to influence her. Best of all, she finds, is the sense of community that has developed in southern Ontario between chefs and growers, particularly because of Knives and Forks.*

# Curried Black Bean and Plantain Soup

ALLI MILLAR
Martin's Catering
*North York, Ontario*

SERVES 6

| | | |
|---|---|---|
| 2 cups | black beans | 500 mL |
| 2 | bay leaves | 2 |
| 3 | lime leaves (optional) | 3 |
| 1 | stem lemon grass, sliced | 1 |
| 3 | large cloves garlic, halved | 3 |
| 2 | slices fresh ginger root | 2 |
| ⅓ cup | olive oil | 75 mL |
| 2 | cooking onions, finely chopped | 2 |
| 1 | small piece fresh ginger root, sliced | 1 |

| | | |
|---|---|---|
| 4 | cloves garlic, peeled and finely chopped | 4 |
| 1½ Tbsp | ground cumin seed | 20 mL |
| 2 tsp | ground coriander seed | 10 mL |
| 1 tsp | ground turmeric | 5 mL |
| 6 cups | chicken stock or water | 1.5 L |
| 2 | stems fresh oregano | 2 |
| 2 | stems fresh thyme | 2 |
| 1 | delicata squash, peeled, cored, halved, and cut into chunks (if unavailable, butternut or other winter squash maybe substituted) | 1 |
| 1 | plantain | 1 |
| 2 | lemons | 2 |
| 1 | bunch fresh coriander, stemmed and chopped | 1 |
| 1 tsp | chili oil or 1 dried red chili pepper or 1 fresh thai chili, chopped | 5 mL |

• Rinse black beans in a colander until rinsing water runs clear. Soak overnight in 4 cups water. Discard any leftover water in the morning.

• Cover the beans with 1½ times their volume of water. Bring to a boil. Skim. Add bay leaves, lime leaves, lemon grass, garlic and 2 slices of ginger root. Simmer for about 40 minutes, until the beans are plump and soft.

• Heat olive oil in a heavy, 2-quart/2 L saucepan and sauté onions over medium heat. Add remaining ginger and garlic and continue stirring until slightly browned. Add cumin seed, coriander seed and turmeric and cook, stirring, about 30 seconds, until colour darkens.

• Pour in chicken stock and continue to boil. Skim. Add oregano, thyme, chunky cut squash and beans. Bring to a boil and reduce heat. Simmer until squash is cooked through, approximately 5 minutes.

• Meanwhile, peel plantain and slice into rounds. Grill, turning once, on a grill or under a broiler. Season with sea salt and freshly ground pepper and the juice of 2 lemons.
• Add plantain to soup and bring to a boil.
• Add chopped coriander and bring to a boil.
• Add chilies. Simmer 5 minutes and serve.

Delicata squash may be obtained from Poplar Lane Farm, St. Lawrence Market, Toronto, (north side, Saturdays only). Fresh herbs are available from Ivanhoe Gardens. Black beans can be purchased at most health food stores. (*See Source Information at back of book.*)

*Fava beans are cool season shelling beans, closely resembling the more common lima bean, that are eaten fresh or dried for future use. Ancient Romans relied on the starchy, broad bean as one of their staples, and modern Italians particularly enjoy the bean's sweet flavour when harvested very young.*

*As I am a true bean lover, the day I received this recipe I began wondering where I might find some of these prized legumes. The next day I happened to be driving west on Major Mackenzie Drive near Highway 400 (just north of Toronto) when I passed two small Italian farms, both of which had signs reading "favas" out by the road. I immediately pulled into one farm, and casually asked the woman behind the counter if the beans were organic. Seeing that she did not fully understand what I said, I asked, "Do you use any insecticides or chemicals on them?" Shaking her head firmly, she smiled and replied, "Oh, definitely not."*

*I left laden with a big bag of the gorgeous, rich legumes, which I nibbled on during the drive back to Toronto. When I got home, I harvested a few carrots and tomatoes from my own garden, put up a large pot of this soup, and that evening my family and I sat down to one of the tastiest meals we could ever remember.*

# Lamb and Tomato Soup with Fava Beans and Gremolata

KEITH FROGGETT
Scaramouche
*Toronto, Ontario*

SERVES 6

| | | |
|---|---|---|
| 2 Tbsp | olive oil | 25 mL |
| 2¼ lbs | lamb shanks | 1 kg |
| 2 | celery stalks, diced | 2 |
| 2 | red onions, diced | 2 |
| 2 | carrots, diced | 2 |
| 4 | large tomatoes, peeled, seeded and diced, juice reserved | 4 |
| 1 Tbsp | balsamic vinegar | 15 mL |

*The following 3 ingredients, tied in a bundle*

| | | |
|---|---|---|
| 12 | cloves garlic | 12 |
| 4 | parsley sprigs | 4 |
| 4 | sprigs thyme | 4 |
| | water | |
| 1½ lbs | fresh fava beans, shelled, blanched, and shelled again (the bean's outer skin slips off easily after blanching) (yields about 1–1½ cups/ 250–375 mL) | 750 g |
| | extra-virgin olive oil | |

### *Gremolata*

*Combine in a small bowl*

| | | |
|---|---|---|
| ¼ cup | chopped parsley | 50 mL |
| 1 | clove garlic, chopped | 1 |
| | zest of ½ lemon | |

• Heat the olive oil in a large pot and brown the lamb shanks all over. Remove. Add the vegetables and brown lightly. Add the tomato juice and the diced tomato. Add vinegar, garlic and herbs, place the shanks on top and cover with water.
• Bring to a boil, then turn down to a bare simmer. Cook for about 2 hours, then remove the garlic–herb bundle. Increase heat and boil for 15 minutes, skimming as required.
• Pull the shank meat from the bone, add the meat back to the soup along with the fava beans, correct the seasoning and flavour with extra-virgin olive oil and gremolata.

*Bryan Steele, of The Old Prune, credits the great German chef Vincent Klink, with whom he worked for four years, as a major influence in his approach to food. Like Klink, Steele relies on many local farmers to supply him with ingredients for his menu, which changes throughout the season. "Most of our suppliers are organic," says Steele, "although many are so small they haven't bothered to become certified. Organic produce is consistently more flavourful," he adds. "When you start with really good-tasting, wholesome ingredients, you don't have to do that much to them."*

*The Old Prune started as a tearoom in the mid 1970s and gradually evolved into a classical French restaurant. Since Steele took over in the kitchen in 1988, the menu has come to reflect his great gift for innovation and a variety of culinary influences.*

# Green Pea Soup with Chicken Liver Dumplings

BRYAN STEELE
The Old Prune
*Stratford, Ontario*

SERVES 4

***Dumplings***

| | | |
|---|---|---|
| ½ lb | fresh chicken livers | 250 g |
| 1 slice | day-old white bread, without crusts, cut into small cubes | 1 slice |
| ½ cup | milk, lukewarm | 125 mL |
| 1 | sprig fresh tarragon | 1 |
| 2 | eggs | 2 |
| 1 Tbsp | unsalted butter | 15 mL |
| 1 Tbsp | vegetable oil | 15 mL |
| | salt, pepper, and freshly-grated nutmeg | |
| | freshly-grated bread crumbs for breading | |

*Soup*

| | | |
|---|---|---|
| 2¼ lbs | fresh shelling peas, preferably young and tender | 1 kg |
| 1 | small onion, minced | 1 |
| 4 cups | water | 1 L |
| 1 cup | 35% cream, brought to a boil and simmered over low heat until reduced by half, about 5 minutes (approximately ½ cup/ 125 mL of reduced cream) | 250 mL |
| 1 Tbsp | 35% cream, whipped | 15 mL |
| 4 | sprigs fresh chervil | 4 |
| | salt, pepper, freshly grated nutmeg, and a few drops of lemon juice for seasoning | |

*Dumplings*

• Preheat oven to 425°F/220°C. Soak the bread cubes in the warm milk. Add the tarragon and seasonings. Cover and allow to steep for 15 minutes. Squeeze the excess moisture from the bread and discard the liquid.

• Chop the livers finely either by hand or use a food processor if desired, and mix together with the soaked bread. Add 1 whole egg and 1 egg yolk to the mixture, reserving the white for later. Check the seasoning and adjust if necessary. Refrigerate the mixture for at least 2 hours before shaping the dumplings.

• When chilled, shape the liver mixture into small, egg-shaped dumplings using a small spoon. Beat the remaining egg white for a few seconds, until just starting to froth. Dip the dumplings into the egg white, then in the fresh bread crumbs to coat. Refrigerate until ready to cook.

*Soup*

• Shell the peas, reserving both peas and pods. Transfer the pods to a narrow pot, add the onion, a good pinch of salt, and cover with the water. Bring to a boil, then reduce heat to low and simmer the stock for 25–30 minutes.

• Remove from heat and purée the mixture in a food processor or blender. Pass the mixture through a fine sieve to remove any fibrous particles.

• Heat the butter and oil together in a heavy skillet. When hot add the breaded dumplings. Transfer to a hot (425°F/220°C) oven and cook for 6–7 minutes, turning once after 4 minutes. When cooked, drain on paper towels to remove excess fat. Keep warm.

• Heat pea stock, reduced cream, seasonings and the shelled peas together, bringing to a simmer. Simmer for exactly 1 minute — no longer. Remove from heat and purée in a blender until smooth. Return to stockpot and heat. Taste for seasoning and adjust if necessary.

• Just before serving, stir in the 1 Tbsp/15 mL whipped cream. Ladle into warm soup bowls and garnish with the chicken liver dumplings and a sprig of fresh chervil.

*"Most culinary cultures are based on predictable repetitions of ingredients," says master gardener Sinclair Philip of B.C.'s legendary Sooke Harbour House. "Traditionally people experienced the pleasure that results from delaying gratification, from anticipating something and then savouring it." Over the last decade Philip, a marine biologist who holds a Ph.D. in economics from the University of Grenoble, has been a significant catalyst behind the development of a regional Pacific Northwest cuisine in British Columbia.*

*Sooke Harbour House lies some thirty-five miles north of Victoria on Vancouver Island, a group of pastoral, charming white cottages that sprawl across a bluff overlooking the Juan de Fuca Straits, just across from Washington State. A profusion of edible flower, herb and vegetable gardens surround the inn, inspiring a cuisine in which seasonal means daily, freshness means seafood that has been harvested by Philip just hours before dinnertime and vegetables that "taste like they're still growing." The restaurant is world renowned for serving some of the most innovative, sophisticated and delicious regional cuisine imaginable, using a range of ingredients wider than perhaps anywhere else in Canada.*

*Philip is outspoken on the subject of food quality in Canada, noting that historically, cooking technique was regarded as an important skill, and was passed on from one generation to the next. With the pervasion of imported, fast foods and prepared foods in our culture, he says, we have lost the ability to create a cuisine based on local and regional ingredients. The average person consumes excessive amounts of sugar, alcohol, inorganic beef, chicken and few, if any vegetables, with the exception of potatoes, and very few seafood products, most of which are processed and/or frozen.*

# Sooke Harbour House Dungeness Crab and Hubbard Squash Consommé

DAVID FEYS
Sooke Harbour House
*Sooke, British Columbia*

SERVES 4-6

| | | |
|---|---|---|
| 6 cups | good-quality, clear rabbit or chicken stock | 1.5 L |
| 2 | live dungeness or red rock crabs | 2 |
| 1 cup | finely chopped carrot | 250 mL |
| 1 cup | finely chopped onion | 250 mL |
| 1 cup | finely chopped celery | 250 mL |
| 1 cup | finely chopped hubbard squash, flesh only | 250 mL |
| 1 cup | finely chopped fennel bulb | 250 mL |
| 5 | egg whites | 5 |
| 3 | juniper berries, crushed | 3 |
| 6 | peppercorns, crushed | 6 |
| 1 tsp | caraway seed | 5 mL |
| ½ cup | finely chopped savoury herbs, i.e., rosemary, sage, flat-leafed parsley and fennel | 125 mL |
| | optional ingredients: | |
| | low sodium tamari sauce, for seasoning | |

***Garnish ingredients***

| | | |
|---|---|---|
| 4 | pincer claws, reserved from crabs | 4 |
| 1 tsp | finely chopped shallots | 5 mL |
| ⅓ cup | white wine or vermouth | 75 mL |

• In a 2-quart/2-litre saucepan, heat stock to boiling and set aside.
• Over a sink, split crabs in half to kill. Remove gills, stomach and coral. Remove pincer claws, refrigerate and reserve for the garnish. Crush crab bodies in a lint-free towel with a mallet or hammer.
• Place crushed crab meat and the shells in a stainless steel mixing bowl. Add chopped vegetables, herbs, juniper berries, peppercorns, caraway seeds, herbs and egg whites. Stir well to mix evenly.
• In a 4-quart/4-litre saucepan set over high heat, place vegetable–crab mixture and, while stirring constantly, add heated stock gradually.
• Reduce heat to medium and carefully stir occasionally to ensure that nothing sticks to the bottom. When a raft (coagulated vegetable and crab mixture) starts to form, stop stirring. Be patient, the process will take approximately 15 minutes. Turn heat down so that a slow simmer is achieved.
• The consommé should cook for approximately 45 minutes to one hour after the raft has formed. Be sure not to boil rapidly or the raft will separate and you will have a complete mess! The raft will feel firm to the touch, not soft and mushy.
• Remove from the heat and, with a ladle, transfer stock into another pot through a cheesecloth-lined strainer. Discard raft.
• Adjust for seasoning with tamari, if desired, and serve at once, or cool, chill and reheat when needed.

### *Garnish*

Preheat oven to 375°F/190°C. Heat a 1-quart/1-litre saucepan with a lid and in it place the crab claws, shallots and the wine. Cover and steam in the oven for 4 minutes. Remove pot from the oven. Garnish the soup with the crab claws and serve immediately.

*EastWest is a natural/macrobiotic foods and lifestyle centre offering counselling, professional training and cooking classes in Toronto's Annex neighbourhood. The macrobiotic philosophy entails eating locally grown, organic foods (whole grains, vegetables, fruits and fish) as much as possible, while avoiding sugar, dairy, eggs and animal protein. Director Malca Narrol has been teaching the principles and techniques of macrobiotics at the centre for ten years. "We encourage people to eat organically-grown foods for environmental reasons, and because they contain more natural vitamins," says Narrol. "The word 'marobiotic' tends to be somewhat intimidating to those who don't fully understand it," she adds. "In fact, even today there remains some confusion as to the difference between organic and macrobiotic."*

*Organic simply refers to the way in which something is grown, while macrobiotic encompasses a whole lifestyle that is aimed at prolonging a more healthful life. With today's widespread concern about the relationship between diet and lifestyle, many of the principles of macrobiotics (particularly the avoidance of animal products and butterfats) have been proven to be quite sound.*

*Quinoa, (pronounced* keen-wa*) an ancient grain from the Andes, has recently achieved popularity as one of the new "supergrains," due to it having more protein, and higher-quality protein, than any other grain. Make sure you rinse the quinoa thoroughly before cooking — or a bitter taste will mar its otherwise delicate flavour.*

# Pinto Bean and Quinoa Soup

MALCA NARROL
EastWest
*Toronto, Ontario*

SERVES 6

| | | |
|---|---|---|
| ¾ cup | organic dried pinto beans | 175 mL |
| 8 cups | water | 2 L |
| 3-inch strip | kombu (a sea vegetable) | 7-cm strip |

| | | |
|---|---|---|
| ½ | onion, diced | ½ |
| ¾ cup | diced butternut or buttercup squash, unpeeled (in summer substitute corn kernels and put the cobs in the stock) | 175 mL |
| ⅓ cup | diced carrot | 75 mL |
| ⅓ cup | diced celery | 75 mL |
| 1–1½ tsp | mixed dried herbs* | 5–7 mL |
| ⅓ cup | quinoa | 75 mL |
| 1¼ tsp | japanese plum paste, to taste** | 6 mL |
| | parsley or cilantro, minced, to garnish | |

• Sort beans for stones. Wash, drain and bring to a boil in 8 cups/2 L of water with the kombu strip. Gently boil for 5 minutes, skimming any foam off the surface.
• Add onions and cook about 5 minutes, until they smell sweet.
• Reduce heat to a simmer and add the remaining vegetables, skimming foam whenever necessary. Rinse skimmer and return any skimmed-off vegetables to the soup.
• Add 1 tsp/5 mL of herbs to the soup. Cover and simmer for an hour and a half.
• Wash and drain quinoa in a very fine strainer. Add to the soup along with another 1 tsp/5 mL of herbs. Cover and simmer at least 30 minutes until beans are very soft. This may take as long as an hour.
• Season with the plum paste, to taste, by diluting small amounts of paste in small amounts of broth in a separate bowl and adding back to the soup. Simmer another 10 minutes.
• Garnish with parsley or cilantro (lots!)

*Note*: Presoaked beans cook faster.

Organic dried pinto beans, kombu, and quinoa can be found at Baldwin Natural Foods and Noah's Natural Foods, Toronto. (*See Source Information at back of book.*)

* Narrol uses an organic blend called "Soup Herbs" that you can order from Meadowbrook Herb Garden, Wyoming, Rhode Island, 02898, U.S.A. It contains basil, celery, parsley, marjoram, thyme, savory and bay leaves, or, you can use your own mix of fresh and/or dried herbs.
**Ohsawa brand is organic but hard to find.

*"It's hard to understand why the North American market has become hooked on those little white button mushrooms," says John Rowe (no relation to the John Rowe of Rowe Farm Meats in Guelph) of Bioharvest in Ancaster, Ontario. "They're harvested two or three days before they are fully ripened, and consequently are too hard and quite flavourless when sold." Rowe's company grows oyster, coral and shiitake mushrooms organically, for sale to the restaurant market.*

*Cultivated mushrooms are grown in a mixture of horse manure and other ingredients, which is then pasteurized to kill any pathogens that may remain in the soil. Insecticides such as Malathion are generally sprayed on the mushrooms as they develop to inhibit the growth of undesirable organisms.*

*Rowe initially tried using this technique to grow the more unusual varieties of mushrooms, but without success. "With pasteurization it is hard to suppress the growth of other organisms without using fungicides," Rowe explains. "This led us to develop a slightly different method: we make up a synthetic wood log using sawdust and other organic supplements, like bran and bone meal; then we pack the mix into plastic bags, and steam sterilize (a process that is similar to canning) the mixture at 250°F/120°C. This kills* absolutely everything *in the mixture. We introduce the starter culture under sterile conditions, and because the mushrooms develop in a protected environment we never have to apply any chemicals."*

*For now, Rowe has all the business he can handle, selling to distributors who in turn sell his products to restaurants. But he looks forward to the day when the consumer will be able to find the more unusual and flavourful shiitake, oyster and coral mushrooms in the supermarket produce department right alongside those little white buttons.*

*As chef de cuisine for Toronto's famed O'Keefe Centre, Kenneth Peace is responsible for organizing many banquets and fund-raising galas. To this he brings extensive experience, having cooked at hotels, on cruise ships and clubs as far away as New South Wales.*

*A founding member of Knives and Forks, Peace became informed about local and organic ingredients through his association with*

*Jamie Kennedy and Michael Stadtlander. He has incorporated many local organic suppliers into the restaurant's regular menu, and often uses them, budget permitting, for large functions.*

# Wild Mushroom Soup with Tarragon and Chives

KENNETH PEACE
O'Keefe Centre
*Toronto, Ontario*

SERVES 6

| | | |
|---|---|---|
| ¼ cup | unsalted butter | 50 mL |
| 4 Tbsp | diced shallots | 50 mL |
| 4 oz | shiitake mushrooms | 125 g |
| 4 oz | cremini mushrooms | 125 g |
| 3 oz | oyster (or coral) mushrooms | 125 g |
| 1 oz | woodear mushrooms | 30 g |
| 2 Tbsp | tarragon leaves, chopped | 25 mL |
| 4 Tbsp | white flour | 50 mL |
| 6 cups | chicken or vegetable stock | 1.5 L |
| 1 Tbsp | chives, chopped | 15 mL |
| | salt, crushed black peppercorns | |
| | tarragon sprigs for garnish | |

- Wash, then slice all mushrooms, approximately ⅛ inch/2 mm thick.
- Melt butter in a saucepan, sauté shallots over medium heat until transparent.
- Add mushrooms and tarragon leaves and continue to sauté until most of the liquid has evaporated.
- Slowly sprinkle flour over mushroom-shallot mixture, stirring constantly, and cook for 5 minutes over medium heat.

- Add cold stock, mix well, and bring to a boil over medium heat. Reduce heat and simmer for approximately 1 hour.
- Season to taste with salt and pepper.
- Serve with chopped chives on top of soup.
- Garnish with tarragon sprig.

Wild mushrooms are available from Oishi Mushrooms in Claremont, Ontario. (*See Source Information at back of book.*)

*Toronto diners who recall with delight the glory of Fenton's will be greatly heartened to learn that after selling the restaurant in 1989, the team of Nicholas Pearce, Allan Barrett and chef Werner Bassen took up residence in a picturesque old house in Wolfville, Nova Scotia. It is there, amidst the bustling Acadia University community, that the three carry on the horticultural/culinary tradition with which they helped to launch the gastronomic revolution in Toronto in the late 1970s.*

*On their own nearby farm, the owners raise herbs, lettuces, strawberries, and an abundance of cutting flowers, which beautify the sixty-seat restaurant in characteristic style. The winter in Wolfville is "much like Ontario's," but perhaps a bit longer. Indeed, it must be, for on the particular day in mid-May when I called, Nicholas Pearce had just finished shovelling a little snow off the lawn. Seasonal vegetables mean jerusalem artichokes, obtained from a nearby member of the local organic growers association, which Bassen offers puréed and delicately flavoured with a bit of freshly-grated nutmeg.*

# Purée of Jerusalem Artichoke Soup

WERNER BASSEN
Acton's Grill and Café
*Wolfville, Nova Scotia*

SERVES 4

| | | |
|---|---|---|
| 1½ lbs | jerusalem artichokes, scrubbed and rinsed, cut in half | 750 g |
| 4 cups | chicken stock | 1 L |
| 1 cup | 35% cream | 250 mL |
| pinch | freshly grated nutmeg | pinch |
| | salt | |
| | white pepper, freshly ground | |

• Combine chicken stock and artichokes and simmer for 20 minutes or until very tender. Remove from heat. Strain liquid into another sauce pan, reserving artichokes.
• Purée artichokes in a food processor and return to the stock. Add the 35% cream and carefully heat, just to boiling. Season with salt and pepper.
• Pour into soup tureen or onto soup plates and top with freshly grated nutmeg just before serving.

Acton's obtains jerusalem artichokes from Norland Farms, Port Williams, Nova Scotia. (*See Source Information at back of book.*)

*A professor of culinary arts at St. Clair College in Windsor, Ontario, as well as a chef and caterer, Glen Van Blommesteim has a unique opportunity to work with locally-grown ingredients while also educating future cooks about some of the benefits of using such products. "I try to use as many organic and locally-grown products as possible," says the genial Van Blommesteim, who runs Overtures, a bistro-style restaurant just outside of Windsor, "I much prefer their taste, and I like to support the local economy." One of his favourite sources of unusual produce is local grower Nancy Burgess, in neighbouring Harrow, who cultivates herbs and gourmet vegetables exclusively for restaurants.*

*"Essex County," says Burgess' partner Scott Martin, "is one of the best-kept secrets in Ontario — or all of Canada, for that matter. As the southernmost county in the southernmost province we get more summer heat, more hours of sunlight, than anywhere else in eastern Canada, and the water that completely surrounds us has a considerable mellowing effect. Burgess' garden abounds with the season's best from early spring until late fall: beginning with her colourful frilly lettuces, to her sweet, thin-skinned eggplants and yellow tomatoes of summer, to the Chinese greens and flowering kales that she harvests when the weather turns cool.*

# Velouté of Butternut Squash with Mixed Herb Pesto

GLEN VAN BLOMMESTEIM
Overtures
*Tecumseh, Ontario*

SERVES 8

| | | |
|---|---|---|
| ⅔ cup | finely chopped shallots | 150 mL |
| 3 Tbsp | butter | 50 mL |
| 1 Tbsp | unbleached flour | 15 mL |
| 2 lbs | butternut squash, peeled, seeded and diced | 1 kg |

| | | |
|---|---|---|
| 8 cups | fresh chicken stock | 2 L |
| ½ cup | 10% cream | 125 mL |
| 2 Tbsp | mixed herb pesto (recipe follows) | 25 mL |
| | salt and freshly ground black pepper | |

### *Mixed Herb Pesto*

| | | |
|---|---|---|
| 1 cup | fresh basil | 250 mL |
| ½ cup | fresh summer savory | 125 mL |
| ½ cup | fresh lavender | 125 mL |
| ¼ cup | chopped fresh garlic | 50 mL |
| ¼ cup | fresh tarragon | 50 mL |
| 1 cup | grated romano cheese | 250 mL |
| ½ cup | pine nuts | 125 mL |
| 1½ cups | extra-virgin olive oil | 375 mL |

- In a large saucepan, sauté shallots in butter until soft and glossy. Add the flour and stir well.
- Add the squash and chicken stock. Simmer until squash is very tender, stirring occasionally.
- When tender, purée the soup until smooth with an immersion blender or pass through a food mill. Return to heat.
- Add herb pesto and cream. Stir gently.
- Adjust seasoning with salt and pepper.
- Serve in large soup plates with herbed croutons and chive flowers.

### *Mixed Herb Pesto*

In a food processor, process all ingredients to a smooth consistency. Store in a sealed jar.

Overtures obtains herbs and squashes from Burgess and Martin Organic Farms, Harrow, Ontario. They do not sell to the public but you can purchase some of their produce at Cream of the Crop in Waterloo, and they will ship to restaurants anywhere in Canada via Priority Post. (*See Source Information at back of book.*)

# SALADS

*South Gillies, Ontario, a small town some forty miles from Thunder Bay, is not where you would expect to find a preponderance of organic food, let alone some of the best cooking in Canada. And yet The Unicorn Inn, "the tiny restaurant at the end of the universe," as affectionately described by its chef and proprietor, David Nobel, has consistently earned accolades in both* Where to Eat in Canada, *the national independent guide to dining that is this country's equivalent of the* Guide Michelin, *and* The Best Places to B&B in Ontario. *David Nobel, a professional baker by training, and his wife Arlan, spent more than two years personally restoring their romantic, turn-of-the-century farmhouse — which lies nestled in a secluded valley amid 440 acres of spectacular scenery — before officially opening in 1979.*

*Despite the unique challenges their location presents, the Nobels are staunchly committed to finding the best ingredients available, and use as much premium local produce, including eggs, vegetables and herbs, as they can obtain. During the growing season, much of their produce is provided especially for them by local growers with whom they work closely. During the winter, this process often entails sitting down together and mapping out a strategy for the coming season, evaluating past successes and failures, poring over seed catalogues, and deciding which new varieties to experiment with.*

*David Nobel is proud to support this region's organic growers, noting, "It is now well established that wherever you find small restauranteurs committed to culinary excellence, you will find demand for organic produce. This is simply because the very best produce is almost invariably organic."*

# Unicorn Inn House Salad

DAVID NOBEL
The Unicorn Inn
*South Gillies, Ontario*

SERVES 4

| | | |
|---|---|---|
| 4 | large handfuls mixed fresh garden greens: i.e. mâche, rocket, red and green leaf, red and green romaine, washed, sorted and dried | 4 |
| 1 Tbsp | red wine vinegar | 15 mL |
| ¼ Tbsp | balsamic vinegar | 10 mL |
| dab | strong dijon mustard | dab |
| dab | tamari (soy sauce) | dab |
| 1½ tsp | sifted grated parmesan cheese | 10 mL |
| ½ cup | extra-virgin olive oil | 125 mL |
| 3 Tbsp | walnut oil (preferably from France) | 50 mL |
| 1½ tsp | chopped or snipped fresh herbs (parsley, dill, chervil, chives, or a combination) | 25 mL |
| | coarse kosher salt or sea salt, and freshly ground black pepper | |
| 12 | thin slices english cucumber | 12 |
| 8 | thin, julienne slices of sweet red pepper | 8 |
| 4 | or more edible flower blossoms (i.e., nasturiums, day lilies, borage, etc.), to garnish | 4 |

• Carefully rip the lettuce into relatively large pieces; small pieces of delicate leaves tend to become sodden quickly when the vinaigrette is added. Place in a large bowl. Cover tightly and refrigerate while making the dressing.

• In a medium-sized bowl, whisk together the wine vinegar, balsamic vinegar, mustard, soy sauce and parmesan cheese.

• Measure the oils together into a container with a spout or pouring lip.

• Immediately before serving, remove the greens from the refrigerator and uncover. Very gradually whisk all the oil into the vinegar mixture until completely homogenized. While still whisking, pour the dressing over the greens, making sure to distribute evenly. You may wish to hold back some dressing until the first addition is mixed, to avoid drowning the salad; add more only if necessary. Sprinkle in half the herbs, throw in a small pinch of salt, and toss thoroughly till just mixed. Adjust the salt and pepper.

• Divide the salad among 4 plates. Garnish each portion with 2 slices of peppers, 3 slices of cucumber, and 1 or more flowers. Finish with a light sprinkle of the remaining herbs, and serve immediately.

*Note:* Some herbs can be torn up relatively large and added directly to the salad leaves — dill and chervil are nice this way. So is basil, and small leaves may be tossed in whole. This salad is very flexible — it lends itself well to various additions and substitutions of oils (hazelnut, mustard); vinegars (sherry, champagne, tarragon); and herbs and greens.

The restaurant obtains its salad greens from Ted Horychuk, a market gardener in Thunder Bay. (*See Source Information at back of book.*)

*Karen Barnaby took over the Raintree kitchen at the end of October, 1992, after working just over a year as a consultant for Capers' new takeout area. She is perhaps best known as chef at Toronto's original David Wood Food Shop, where she created the upscale caterer's menus, specials and co-authored* The David Wood Food Book.

*Raintree was designed to be a model of environmental responsibility, and challenges other restaurants and businesses to also adopt environmentally responsible practices. Food, first and foremost, is locally-produced and in season, to reflect the abundant environment of British Columbia. Preference is given to food grown in a sustainable manner with minimal pesticides and natural fertilizers wherever possible. The three Rs of waste management — Reduce, Reuse and Recycle, are firmly entrenched in the restaurant's daily operation: all glass, cardboard, plastic, paper, cans and oils are recycled. And recycled paper is used exclusively for all printing, including menus, stationery and promotional materials while recycled, unbleached paper products are used for such items as coffee filters and toilet paper. Raintree hosts and participates in fund-raising benefits for hunger relief and environmental causes, and donates excess food to Food Runners, a local food recovery program that redistributes surplus food to shelters, soup kitchens and missions in the greater Vancouver area.*

*Like Alice Waters, one of our generation's greatest proponents of seasonal and regional cuisine, restaurant co-owner and general manager Janice Lotzkar also believes that food should be experienced through the senses, and not frozen, hermetically sealed or manipulated so as to withstand transportation over great distances. "One of the greatest challenges facing contemporary chefs," she notes, "is the development of a cuisine based on products with extremely short growing seasons, while still remaining true to our regional offerings."*

*In recent years, the Pacific Northwest has gained widespread recognition for its great variety of indiginous foods. At Raintree, the quest to explore this region's culinary roots becomes an exhilarating adventure incorporating the coastal waters of the Pacific, and the local wineries and farms, throughout the ever-changing seasons.*

# Beet, Fennel and Apple Salad

KAREN BARNABY
Raintree Restaurant
*Vancouver, British Columbia*

SERVES 4

| | | |
|---|---|---|
| 1 lb | small beets, cooked and peeled | 454 g |
| 1 | medium bulb fennel, stalks removed, trimmed, with the tender, inner green fronds saved | 1 |
| 1 | small apple, peeled and cored | 1 |

*Dressing*

| | | |
|---|---|---|
| 4 | shallots, peeled and sliced | 4 |
| 1 Tbsp | dijon mustard | 15 mL |
| ½ tsp | salt | 2 mL |
| 1 Tbsp | apple cider vinegar | 15 mL |
| 1 Tbsp | honey | 15 mL |
| ½ cup | cold-pressed vegetable oil | 125 mL |
| 1 Tbsp | coarsely chopped dill | 15 mL |

• Cut the beets in half lengthwise and slice into ⅓-inch/8-mm slices. Place in a bowl. Slice the fennel in half lengthwise and core. Cut crosswise into ¼-inch/6-mm slices. Coarsely chop the tender greens. Add to the beets. Cut the apple into ½-inch/1-cm cubes. Add to the beets.

### *Dressing*

• Place the shallots, dijon mustard, salt, apple cider vinegar and honey in the workbowl of a good processor or blender. Turn the machine on and add the oil in a slow thin stream. Add the dill and pulse once. Pour over the beet mixture and stir to combine.

*A few miles south of Nanaimo, B.C., just across the Nanaimo River Bridge and off the beaten path, lies a restaurant well worth seeking out: The Old Mahle House. Maureen Loucks and her brother-partner Delbert purchased the weathered country house in 1984, and since then, their imaginative, locally-based cuisine has delighted guests from near and far. The Loucks partially attribute their success to their diligent search for quality ingredients, which are often organic. "Organic producers have a difficult time making a living," says Maureen, "and any support we can give them is definitely worth the effort."*

*The Old Mahle House is fortunate to be situated within close proximity of a number of small farms. They also have their own garden from which they obtain some of the produce and fresh herbs which are used in the restaurant. Right down the road lies the Hazelwood Herb Farm, which has one of the most extensive ranges of herbs grown anywhere in Canada.*

# Red and Yellow Tomato Salad with Thai Basil Dressing

MAUREEN LOUCKS
The Old Mahle House
*Cedar, British Columbia*

SERVES 4

| | | |
|---|---|---|
| 1 | head radicchio | 1 |
| 2 | ripe red tomatoes | 2 |
| 2 | ripe yellow tomatoes | 2 |
| ¼ cup | roasted pine nuts | 50 mL |

***Dressing***

| | | |
|---|---|---|
| 1 | egg | 1 |
| 2 tsp | dijon mustard | 10 mL |
| 2 Tbsp | white wine vinegar | 25 mL |
| 1 cup | olive oil | 250 mL |

| | | |
|---|---|---|
| 2 cups | sour cream | 500 mL |
| 1 Tbsp | fresh lemon juice | 15 mL |
| | large bunch fresh Thai basil, leaves only and several flowers reserved for garnish | |
| | salt and white pepper | |

• Separate radicchio into leaves. Wash and spin dry. Line 4 plates with the radicchio. Slice the tomatoes into thick slices and arrange on top of the radicchio in a circle, alternating colours.

• Top with a dollop of the dressing and sprinkle with roasted pine nuts. Garnish with Thai basil flowers and serve.

### *Dressing*

Mix the egg, dijon mustard and white wine vinegar in a blender and beat until just foamy. Then, with the machine running, add the oil in a thin, steady stream. With the machine still running, add the sour cream, lemon juice and fresh basil, and salt and pepper to taste. Blend just until dressing is a light green colour.

Thai basil can be obtained from Hazelwood Herb Farm, Ladysmith, B.C. Yellow tomatoes (the Old Mahle House uses 'Lemon Boy') are grown by Gary Argyle in Nanaimo, B.C. (*See Source Information at back of book.*)

*A graduate of Montreal's Institute of Hotel and Tourism, Louis Gervais worked in several Montreal restaurants, including Helini, before moving to Vancouver to open the restaurant in the Wedgewood Hotel. When Le Meridien opened in 1985, he joined the staff as sous-chef, and has been there ever since.*

*Local, seasonal ingredients are the hallmark of Gervais' cuisine. "We try to use as many local and seasonal products as possible," he notes, "and, wherever possible, Canadian seafood. We are fortunate to have six varieties of scallops, farmed or from the ocean, to choose from. For this recipe I would use swimming scallops. They are a large ocean scallop with a little bit of roe, and very delicious."*

# Scallop and Cheese Salad with a Garlic and Raspberry Vinaigrette

LOUIS GERVAIS
Le Club Restaurant at Le Meridien Hotel
*Vancouver, British Columbia*

SERVES 6

| | | |
|---|---|---|
| 12 | large ocean scallops, sliced in half (24 pieces) | 12 |
| 6 | handfuls of baby salad greens | 6 |
| ⅓ cup | wiltshire cheese, finely shredded | 90 mL |
| ⅓ cup | emmenthal cheese, finely shredded | 90 mL |
| ⅓ cup | fresh mozzarella cheese, finely shredded | 90 mL |
| 3 | organic tomatoes, cut into chunks | 3 |
| 1¼ cups | garlic and raspberry vinaigrette (recipe follows) | 300 mL |

### *Garlic and Raspberry Vinaigrette*

| | | |
|---|---|---|
| 7 oz | shallots, chopped | 200 g |
| 2 | cloves garlic, purééd | 2 |
| 7 Tbsp | raspberry vinegar | 100 mL |
| ¾ cup | extra-virgin olive oil | 175 mL |
| 5 oz | fresh raspberries | 150 g |

### *Salad*

• Grill the scallops, turning once, on a hot grill or barbecue or broil under a broiler.

• In a bowl mix together the salad greens, the three cheeses and the tomatoes. Toss with the vinaigrette.

• Place salad on plates. Arrange grilled scallops on top of salad and serve.

### *Garlic and Raspberry Vinaigrette*

• Combine first 3 ingredients and mix well.

• Stir in oil until well combined.

• Gently stir in fresh raspberries.

*For chef Neil Baxter of Rundles Restaurant in Stratford, Ontario the re-opening of the restaurant each May, which coincides with the beginning of the acclaimed Stratford Shakespeare Festival is "like opening a new restaurant every year." Amidst an enchanting collection of works by Canadian artist Victor Tinkl, Baxter offers his own form of culinary enchantment, which evolves with the availability of local ingredients throughout the season.*

*Asparagus begins arriving at the kitchen's back door "around Mother's Day and continues until Father's Day." Some of the salad greens come from Cookstown Greens, while other seasonal greens such as chervil, sorrel and watercress come from local farmers who grow them especially for the restaurant.*

*Rundles is open until the end of October. From November through March it plays host to the renowned Stratford Chefs School, which was established in 1983 by several of the town's restaurants in response to the need for locally-trained talent in the culinary arts.*

# Warm Scallop Salad with Artichokes

NEIL BAXTER
Rundles Restaurant
*Stratford, Ontrio*

SERVES 6

| | | |
|---|---|---|
| 12 oz | medium sea scallops | 375 g |
| 1 lb | bunch asparagus | 454 g |
| 12 | baby carrots, peeled, with ½ inch/1 cm green tops left on | 12 |
| 6 | medium artichokes | 6 |
| ½ cup | flour | 125 mL |
| 2 | eggs, lightly beaten | 2 |
| ½ cup | bread crumbs | 125 mL |

***Salad***

| | | |
|---|---|---|
| 2 cups | corn oil | 500 mL |
| 5 Tbsp | olive oil | 65 mL |
| | salt and freshly ground black pepper | |
| 3 | large handfuls mixed lettuces: i.e., tender curly endive, watercress, mâche, bronze leaf, red leaf, chervil, sorrel, etc., washed, dried and refrigerated | 3 |
| ¼ cup | curry oil (recipe follows) | 50 mL |

***Vinaigrette***

| | | |
|---|---|---|
| 1 | shallot, finely chopped | 1 |
| ⅓ cup | sherry vinegar | 75 mL |
| | salt and freshly ground black pepper | |
| 1 cup | olive oil | 250 mL |
| 2 Tbsp | chives, finely chopped | 25 mL |
| 2 Tbsp | tarragon, finely chopped | 25 mL |

***Curry oil***

| | | |
|---|---|---|
| ¼ cup | curry powder | 50 mL |
| 2 Tbsp | cold water | 25 mL |
| 2 cups | canola oil | 500 mL |
| 1 | vanilla bean | 1 |

***Vinaigrette***

• Combine the shallot with the vinegar and add salt and black pepper. Stir in the olive oil. Add the chopped herbs just before serving.

• Prepare the scallops by removing any connective muscle still attached to the side of the scallop, place on shallow plates, cover and refrigerate until later.

• Peel the first ½ inch/1 cm from the base of each asparagus spear, then cut into two pieces. Blanch in boiling salted water for 15 seconds. Drain, rinse in cold water and set aside until later.
• Boil the carrots in salted water until soft. Drain and mix with 2 Tbsp/25 mL of the vinaigrette.
• Trim the artichokes down to the heart, and scoop out the choke, making sure that the artichokes are well rubbed with lemon juice. Bring 4 cups/1 L of lightly salted water to a boil, plunge the artichoke hearts in and cook until just done. Remove from the water, allow to cool slightly, then cut each artichoke heart into 4 slices.
• After completely dry, dip the artichoke hearts in the flour, then in the eggs and finally in the bread crumbs. Store uncovered in one layer in the refrigerator.

### *Salad*

• Heat the corn oil in a deep saucepan. Dress the asparagus with 3 Tbsp/50 mL of the vinaigrette, then season with salt and pepper.
• Lightly flour the scallops. Heat two medium-sized cast iron skillets, divide the 5 Tbsp/65 mL olive oil between the two skillets and allow it to heat. Add the scallops, making sure that they are in one layer. Season with salt and pepper. When golden brown, turn. Continue frying until the second side is the same colour. This should take 2–3 minutes per side.
• Dress the salad greens with the remaining vinaigrette, arrange in the middle of 6 individual serving plates, and place the asparagus and carrots decoratively around the border.
• Deep-fry the artichoke pieces in the corn oil and dry on paper towels, then scatter throughout the salad. Place 5–6 pieces of scallops per plate, decorate the border with the ¼ cup/50 mL curry oil and serve immediately.

### *Curry oil*

• Mix water and curry powder to form a paste. Put the paste into a jar, add the oil and shake well. You may shake several times to increase the strength of the oil. The spice particles will gradually settle to the bottom of the jar. Filter when clear.

• Before using add 1 scraped vanilla bean to curry oil. Shake well and allow to infuse.

Creative Hands Enterprises (Kingview Farms) in Aurora, Ontario and Greyburr Farm in Markdale, Ontario are two sources for excellent asparagus. *(See Source Information at back of book.)*

*From the street, the roof of Vancouver's Pacific Palisades Hotel looks no different from any of the other highrise buildings that surround it. And yet it is here, in the heart of downtown Vancouver, right on the city's fashionable Robson Street, that Executive Chef Anne Milne grows over forty varieties of vegetables and herbs for year-round use in the hotel's Monterey Lounge and Grill. In her "secret" garden, Milne, with the assistance of gardener Dawn Thomson, tends a vegetable patch that includes such hard-to-find varieties as French flageolet beans, edible podded peas, ruby swiss chard, miniature yellow roma tomatoes, and shiso, an herb often used in Japanese cuisine, as well as the many fresh herbs that are the hallmark of Milne's fresh, flavourful cuisine. Arugula, red oak leaf, radicchio and frisée, all of which comprise the hotel's special salad mix, are grown there as well, along with calendulas and nasturtiums — colourful edible flowers whose orange and scarlet petals decorate Milne's innovative summer salads. The sun-warmed herbs even find their way onto Monterey's menus during Vancouver's cold, damp winters: Milne uses basil and rosemary from the garden to flavour oils and infuses vinegars with fresh herbs.*

*Container gardening in the middle of the city presents unique challenges that haven't been easily overcome: "There are environmental stresses," says Thomson, "plants in containers aren't as happy as plants in the good earth." The rooftop garden's soil is composed of organic matter, peat and sand, and a top dressing of worm castings is applied periodically.*

*One of Canada's leading chefs, Anne Milne has an imaginative approach to food that is distinguished by her use of fresh ingredients, simple sauces and a passion for grilling. Her distinctive food style reflects the cuisines of Italy, California, Mexico and the Orient. Her previous restaurant, Café Splash, which she opened in 1986, was an instant success, and brought her widespread recognition.*

# Warmed Canadian Goat Cheese with Arugula and a Sun-dried Tomato Vinaigrette

ANNE MILNE
Monterey Lounge and Grill,
Pacific Palisades Hotel
*Vancouver, British Columbia*

SERVES 4

| | | |
|---|---|---|
| 4 | large handfuls of mixed lettuces | 4 |
| 5 oz | log goat cheese | 150 g |
| several | cracked peppercorns | several |
| 4 Tbsp | sun-dried tomato vinaigrette (recipe follows) | 50 mL |
| | melba toast | |

***Vinaigrette***

| | | |
|---|---|---|
| 1 Tbsp | dijon mustard | 15 mL |
| ½ cup | white wine vinegar | 125 mL |
| to taste | salt and pepper | to taste |
| dash | worcestershire sauce | dash |
| dash | tabasco sauce | dash |
| ½ | shallot | ½ |
| 1 | large clove garlic | 1 |
| 2 cups | mixture of olive and vegetable oil | 500 mL |
| ¼ cup | mixed puréed fresh herbs (basil, thyme, rosemary, parsley) | 50 mL |
| 1 oz | finely chopped sun-dried tomatoes (note: oven-dried tomatoes may be substituted for purchased sun-dried tomatoes) | 30 g |

• Select a variety of lettuces from the garden, including lots of arugula. Wash and spin dry. Arrange attractively on 4 plates.
• Roll goat cheese in cracked peppercorns. Slice into ¼-inch/5-mm coins. Warm in a 350°F/180°C oven for approximately 3–4 minutes, until cheese just starts to melt.
• Place cheese on bed of lettuces.
• Drizzle with vinaigrette.
• Serve with melba toast, preferably homemade.

### *Vinaigrette*

MAKES 3 CUPS/750 ML

• In a large stainless steel bowl, mix mustard, white wine vinegar, salt and pepper, worcestershire sauce and tabasco.
• In a food processor, process shallot and garlic. Add vinegar and mustard mixture.
• With machine on, slowly drizzle oil into mixture in a slow, steady stream. Season to taste.
• Stir in herbs and sun-dried tomatoes by hand.

*In the five years since David Cohlmeyer and his wife Barbara established Cookstown Greens on a seven-acre organic farm and greenhouse complex just an hour north of Toronto, they have become the area's leading producer of top quality specialty produce for restaurants and hotels. Prior to founding the company, Cohlmeyer was a well-known figure in the Toronto food scene for more than fifteen years.*

*The Cohlmeyers are perhaps best known for their distinctive mix of baby salad greens, which are chosen as much for their fascinating appearance as for their luscious flavour. Cookstown Greens are comprised of about thirty-five different ingredients, including a dozen varieties of baby lettuces, lemony purslane and sorrel, amaranth, lamb's quarters, nasturtium, mustard leaves and wild shepherd's purse, into which are sprinkled a burst of colourful edible flower petals. These hand-picked delicacies are thoroughly cleaned, spun dry and chilled in large bags for sale to some thirty restaurants around Toronto and Ontario.*

*"We must educate the public to make them realize that organically grown food is worthwhile," says David Cohlmeyer. "Properly grown potatoes demonstrate what a difference organic growing can make. Conventional potato fields are sprayed with herbicides; seed potatoes are dipped in fungicide and developing plants are sprayed with pesticides. This process yields cheap potatoes.*

*Organic potato fields, by contrast, are cultivated to reduce weeds. Healthy soil, beneficial insects and periodic hand-picking keep pests under control. Finally, the potatoes are harvested only after the tops die. This produces potatoes that taste the way potatoes should.*

*As freshness has become the watchword in many restaurants and the chef has become a purveyor of the freshest ingredients available, it is the farmer who is gaining recognition as the culinary hero of the 1990s. In Ontario, David Cohlmeyer is one of a handful of local growers providing both chefs and the public a connection with the land and firsthand knowledge about food and how it is grown.*

# Potato Salad

DAVID COHLMEYER
Cookstown Greens
*Cookstown, Ontario*

SERVES 8

| | | |
|---|---|---|
| 2 lbs | (18 small) whole new or red potatoes | 1 kg |
| ½ cup | cider vinegar | 125 mL |
| 1 tsp | salt | 5 mL |
| ¾ cup | eggless mayonnaise (recipe follows) | 175 mL |

***Eggless Mayonnaise***

| | | |
|---|---|---|
| 3 Tbsp | lemon juice | 50 mL |
| 1 Tbsp | mustard powder | 15 mL |
| 2 | cloves garlic, chopped | 2 |
| pinch | salt | pinch |
| 1 cup | vegetable oil | 250 mL |

• Wash potatoes, then place in a large pot, with larger potatoes on the bottom. Cover with hot water and bring to a simmer. Cook at a simmer only until potatoes have lost their raw crunch (about 20 minutes.)
• Drain promptly. Briefly dip each potato into cold water and cut into bite-sized pieces. Toss the potato pieces with vinegar and salt while they are still hot. Set aside to cool.
• When cooled, toss potatoes with mayonnaise. Potato salad can be served right away but tastes better after marinating for a couple of hours.

## *Eggless Mayonnaise*

YIELDS 1¼ CUPS/300 ML

*Note:* Egg yolks are usually used in commercial mayonnaise because they stabilize the oil of this dressing so well. Whenever their flavours are appropriate, garlic and mustard are good stabilizers too. Do not attempt to reduce this recipe.

• Combine lemon juice, mustard powder, garlic and salt in a blender or food processor. Process until blended.
• With motor running, slowly drizzle in oil. Continue adding the oil, drop by drop, until the mixture has thickened. (All the oil may not be required.)

Filsinger's cider vinegar, from the Filsinger organic orchards of Ayton, Ontario, is available at specialty and natural food stores. (*See Source Information at back of book.*)

# SEAFOOD

# Grilled Loin of Swordfish with Chanterelles

GARY HYNES
Cooper's Inn
*Shelburne, Nova Scotia*

SERVES 4

| | | |
|---|---|---|
| 4 | boneless fillets of swordfish, about 6–8 oz/ 170-225 g each | 4 |
| ½ cup | red wine | 125 mL |
| ½ cup | chicken stock | 125 mL |
| ½ cup | 35% cream | 125 mL |
| 1 cup | fresh chanterelles, picked over, cut in half | 250 mL |
| 1 Tbsp | minced green onions | 15 mL |
| 1 tsp | fresh thyme, chopped | 5 mL |
| 2 strips | nitrate-free bacon, diced, fat rendered | 2 strips |
| 1 | carrot, diced fine, blanched | 1 |
| ½ stalk | celery, diced fine | ½ stalk |
| ½ cup | unsalted butter, chilled | 125 mL |

- Preheat grill or barbecue.
- Place wine, stock, cream, mushrooms, onions, thyme, bacon, carrot and celery in a saucepan and reduce until thick.
- Brush fillets with a little oil and grill until just pink to keep fish juicy.
- Whisk butter into the sauce and pour over swordfish.

*"Cooking is like painting," says Wolfgang von Wieser of the Vancouver Four Seasons Hotel. "The mixing and blending of different colours is a lot like the blending of different national influences to create one's own style." Von Wieser has spent the last six years with the Four Seasons Hotel chain, from 1989 to the present in Vancouver, and from 1986–89 in Toronto. Prior to that he worked at the Dorchester Hotel in England for a year, and spent a memorable year in Monte Carlo.*

*French chefs have very close links with farmers, he says, recalling one incident in which a family for whom he was working picked some tomatoes from the field at 5:00 p.m. and they were "still warm from the field when I put them on the table." The pleasure he experiences from working with something at its peak of flavour is what makes cooking so satisfying for him. "During the summer in Vancouver, we can get whatever we want from local organic farms. During the winter, we have to rely on shipments from California and Mexico — what I call 'truck ripened' produce. It's just not the same at all."*

# Cajun-Grilled Scallops with a Sesame Mayonnaise

WOLFGANG VON WIESER
Four Seasons Hotel
*Vancouver, British Columbia*

SERVES 4

| | | |
|---|---|---|
| 1 | egg yolk | 1 |
| ¾ cup | organic sesame seed oil (Omega brand) | 175 mL |
| 1 Tbsp | white wine vinegar | 15 mL |
| 4 | handfuls of organic salad greens | 4 |
| 24 oz | fresh sea scallops | 750 g |

| | | |
|---|---|---|
| ½ cup | cajun spice | 125 mL |
| 2 Tbsp | olive oil | 25 mL |
| | salt and pepper | |
| | black sesame seeds | |

### *Mayonnaise*

• Place egg yolk in the bowl of a good processor. With motor running, slowly drizzle in sesame seed oil. Gradually add vinegar. If mayonnaise is a little thick add a bit of water until it pours easily from a spoon. Season to taste.

• Prepare greens by washing and removing cores from leaves. Spin dry.
• Place scallops in a small bowl and sprinkle with cajun spice and olive oil. Mix together. Grill scallops on a hot, preheated grill, turning gently until cooked. Season with a pinch of salt.
• Arrange greens on plate. Place scallops on top and drizzle with mayonnaise. Garnish with black sesame seeds.

*"One of the factors impeding the development of a national food style," says Sinclair Philip of Sooke Harbour House, "is that Canadians do not appreciate many of the excellent foods they have and rarely know how to cook with them." For example, stocks of the Northwest abalone were almost depleted before most Canadians even realized what abalone was. A beautiful salt-water marine mollusc with a coiled shell, abalone is harvested by divers on the Pacific coast and sold on a limited basis. Since it is a muscle with no fatty tissue, the meat does not accumulate toxic wastes, bacteria, red tide or heavy metals as do other seafoods.*

*"In Canada," says Philip," we must discard our traditional culinary prejudices and learn to appreciate, protect and make use of the vast variety available to us, if the quality of our food is to improve."*

# Canadian Abalone with Wild Sorrel and Nettle Sauce

SINCLAIR PHILIP
Sooke Harbour House
*Sooke, British Columbia*

SERVES 4

| | | |
|---|---|---|
| 2¼ lbs | fresh abalone, northern or pinto variety | 1 kg |
| 6 Tbsp | unsalted butter, clarified | 100 mL |

***Wild Sorrel and Nettle Sauce***

| | | |
|---|---|---|
| 3 Tbsp | shallots, finely minced | 50 mL |
| 1 | large clove garlic, finely minced | 1 |
| 3 Tbsp | unsalted butter, clarified | 50 mL |
| 24 | wild sorrel leaves | 24 |
| 24 | young nettle leaves (use gloves when handling) | 24 |

| | | |
|---|---|---|
| 2 cups | fish stock | 500 mL |
| ¾ cup | dry white wine | 175 mL |
| 1 cup | 35% cream | 250 mL |
| 3 Tbsp | cold, unsalted butter | 50 mL |

• Use a spoon to remove the muscle from the shell of the abalone. Discard the rest. Place flat side on cutting board and slice it vertically into very thin pieces, approximately ⅛ inch–1/16 inch/2–3 mm. Set aside.
• In a pot, sauté shallots and garlic in clarified butter until soft. Add sorrel and nettles and sauté gently. Add the fish stock and wine and bring to a boil, reducing by half.
• Liquidize in blender then pass through a fine sieve. Pour back into the pot and add cream. Simmer for 5 minutes or until thickened. Remove from heat and whisk in cold butter in small pieces.
• In a frying pan, heat clarified butter over a medium-high heat and sauté abalone lightly on both sides (30–45 seconds, depending on thickness).
• Spoon sauce onto places and arrange abalone attractively. You may garnish with fresh edible flowers such as freesias, calendula, mustard flowers or chickweed flowers.

*Note:* Sooke Harbour House grows its own nettles but they could be gathered in the wild. A member of the mint family, nettles are about 2 ft/60 cm high and have a squarish stem. They are less acidic than french sorrel and are very high in potassium. As the plants are covered with stinging hairs, one must use gloves when picking them.

# Claypot Salmon with Tomato Rosemary Butter Sauce

ANNE MILNE
Monterey Lounge and Grill,
Pacific Palisades Hotel
*Vancouver, British Columbia*

SERVES 4

*For this recipe you will need a clean clay pot and a barbecue or grill.*

| | | |
|---|---|---|
| 4 | skinless and boneless salmon fillets, 5 oz/150 g each | 4 |
| | olive oil | |
| | cracked pepper | |
| | salt | |

***Tomato Rosemary Butter Sauce***

| | | |
|---|---|---|
| ¼ cup | white wine vinegar | 50 mL |
| ¼ cup | dry white wine | 50 mL |
| ¼ cup | finely minced shallot | 50 mL |
| 4 | white peppercorns | 4 |
| pinch | salt | pinch |
| few drops | 35% cream | few drops |
| 1 cup | unsalted butter, cut into 16 pieces, at room temperature | 250 mL |
| few drops | fresh lemon juice | few drops |
| 1 Tbsp | fresh rosemary, finely chopped and blanched | 15 mL |
| 1 | ripe, medium-sized tomato peeled, seeded and finely chopped | 1 |

- Make sure barbecue grill is very clean. Rub with oil, then heat until very hot.

• Rub salmon with olive oil and season with fresh cracked pepper and salt.
• Place fillets on barbecue, skin side up.
• Place clean clay pot over fish. This "smokes" fish and reduces cooking time.
• After 3–4 minutes, turn fish at a 45° angle. Cover with pot and cook for another 3–4 minutes.
• Flip fish and replace pot. Cook fish to desired doneness. (Fish should just lose its transparent look and become translucent).
• Place fish on warmed plate. Nap with sauce.

### *Tomato Rosemary Butter Sauce*

• Heat vinegar, wine, shallot, peppercorns and salt in a small, heavy, noncorrosive saucepan over medium heat and bring to a boil. Reduce heat to very low and simmer until no more than ½ tsp/2mL liquid remains when pan is tilted and the shallot mixture appears as a moist, mushy purée, about 10 minutes.
• Add cream and bring to a boil. Immediately remove from heat; cool slightly.
• Whisk butter, 1 piece at a time, into reduction in saucepan. Add each piece just as the previous one is almost incorporated.
• Move pan on and off very low heat as necessary to maintain smooth but not runny consistency. When all butter is added, you should have a thick, creamy emulsion with no greasy streaks. Add drops of lemon juice to taste; strain into warm sauceboat.
• Add rosemary and tomato. Serve immediately.

Monterey Lounge and Grill uses organically farmed salmon from Yellow Island Aquaculture in Campbell River, British Columbia. *(See Source Information at back of book.)*

*Gary Hynes opened Palmerston with Jamie Kennedy in 1985, where Hynes served as the restaurant's first sommelier. Self-taught, he learned how to cook by observing Kennedy in the restaurant's open kitchen, and naturally "absorbed his philosophy."*

*After leaving Palmerston, Hynes travelled to parts of the world noted for their cuisine: France, Vancouver and San Francisco, among others. Family ties lured him back to Nova Scotia in 1987, and while honeymooning there he and his wife thought running a country inn might be a nice way of life. The beautifully-restored Cooper's Inn, which the Hynes have owned since 1987, has five charming guest rooms and a beautiful view of the sailboats in Shelburne Harbour.*

*Hynes uses a lot of local ingredients in his cooking, "by choice and by necessity. When you're two hours away from the nearest main city you discover the potential in what can be found right around you." Commercial fishing has depleted many species, like cod, and consequently, many local people are now turning to the less popular species like cusk, ocean catfish and hake.*

*A North Atlantic fish, hake is a full-flavoured member of the cod family, popular in Spain and currently gaining popularity in Nova Scotia. Gary Hynes enlivens it with the tartness of local gooseberries, which come from a nearby friend's garden. If gooseberries are not available, apple slices or white grapes would work very nicely.*

# Fillet of Hake with Gooseberries

GARY HYNES
Cooper's Inn
*Shelburne, Nova Scotia*

SERVES 4

| | | |
|---|---|---|
| ½ cup | unsalted butter, chilled | 125 mL |
| 1 Tbsp | light olive oil | 15 mL |

| | | |
|---|---|---|
| 4 | hake fillets, 6 oz/180 g each dredged in flour | 4 |

*Sauce*

| | | |
|---|---|---|
| ½ cup | Ste. Famille Seyval Blanc white wine (a local winery near Wolfville, N.S. Seyval blanc is a white grape unique to the East Coast) | 125 mL |
| 2 Tbsp | rice vinegar | 25 mL |
| 1 cup | fresh gooseberries, picked over | 250 mL |
| 4 tsp | toasted, skinned and split hazelnuts | 20 mL |
| 1 Tbsp | green onions, chopped | 15 mL |
| 4 pinches | chopped lemon thyme | 4 pinches |

- Preheat the oven to 450°F/230°C.
- Heat oil and 1 Tbsp/15 mL butter in a non-stick skillet to just before the smoking point. Place the fillets in the pan and brown lightly. Turn the fillets once and place the pan in the oven for about 5 minutes or until the fish is just done.
- Meanwhile, in another pan, place the wine, vinegar, gooseberries, hazelnuts and onions, and boil until the liquid is reduced to about 1 tsp/5 mL.
- Take off the heat and whisk in the lemon thyme and remaining butter to incorporate and make a creamy sauce.
- Arrange the fillets on plates and top with the sauce.

The restaurant serves this dish with deep fried leeks, an assortment of fresh vegetables and slices of roasted new potatoes tossed in pesto.

*Just north of P.E.I., lie the Îles de la Madeleine, a pastoral group of tiny islands. At La Table des Roy, a pleasant old frame house on the island of Cap aux Meules, Johanne Vigneault offers the best of fresh-caught local seafood and vegetables, in a menu that changes daily throughout the summer season.*

*La Table des Roy was originally Vigneault's family home. In 1978, her parents sold the house to André and Francine Roy, two vacationing restauranteurs who fell in love with the area and wanted to open a restaurant in the islands. The Roys suggested that Vigneault (who was only fourteen at the time) help them out for the season. Johanne Vigneault remained in the house for seven years, diligently absorbing everything the Roys had to teach her. When the Roys decided to return to city life in 1986, Vigneault took the plunge: she bought back her family home and became the restaurant's chef and owner at the mere age of twenty-two! Since then, Vigneault has spent her winters studying cooking and restaurant management with prominent chefs from Québec to France. In June of 1992 she was invited to present the cuisine of the Îles de la Madeleine to a group of patrons of the Musée du Québec.*

# Grilled Herbed Halibut Fillets

JOHANNE VIGNEAULT
Restaurant la Table des Roy
*Cap aux Meules*
*Îles de la Madeleine, Québec*

SERVES 4

| | | |
|---|---|---|
| 4 | halibut fillets, 5 oz/150 g each | 4 |

***Marinade***

| | | |
|---|---|---|
| | juice of 1 lemon | |
| ½ cup | pure olive oil | 125 mL |
| 2 Tbsp | fresh thyme, chopped | 25 mL |
| 2 Tbsp | fresh coriander, coarsely chopped | 25 mL |

| | | |
|---|---|---|
| 4 | leaves fresh basil, finely chopped | 4 |
| 4 | sprigs flat-leafed parsley chopped | 4 |
| | salt and freshly ground pepper | |

***Aromatic oil***

| | | |
|---|---|---|
| | reserved zest of the lemon | |
| 1 cup | pure olive oil | 250 mL |
| ¼ cup | sun-dried tomatoes | 50 mL |
| ¼ cup | black olives, pitted | 50 mL |
| | salt and freshly ground pepper | |
| 4 | basil leaves, finely chopped | 4 |
| 4 | sprigs of flat-leafed parsley, finely chopped | 4 |
| 2 Tbsp | coriander, coarsely chopped | 25 mL |

• Remove the lemon zest and set aside and press out the juice. Combine lemon juice oil, all the herbs, and salt and pepper in a dish large enough to marinate the halibut fillets. Let marinate approximately 2 hours, turning once.
• To prepare the aromatic oil, blanch the lemon zest. Finely chop the tomatoes and olives. Combine all ingredients with the olive oil. Let sit for at least 1 hour before serving to allow flavours to meld.
• When ready to serve, remove the fillets from the marinade and place on absorbent paper to remove as much oil as possible. Sear in a hot skillet, taking care not to overcook. The fish will dry out somewhat during cooking.
• To serve, place the fillets on a hot plate and top with a bit of the aromatic oil.

Johanne Vigneault obtains certified organic lettuces, edible flowers and herbs from Biojardins Plein Sud. She also grows many of the restaurant's herbs in her own garden. *(See Source Information at back of book.)*

# Grilled Salmon with Fresh Corn Sauté and Tomato–Basil Relish

KAREN BARNABY
Raintree Restaurant
*Vancouver, British Columbia*

SERVES 6

| | | |
|---|---|---|
| 6 | spring salmon fillets, 6 oz/175 g each | 6 |
| ½ tsp | salt | 2 mL |
| 1 tsp | freshly ground black pepper | 5 mL |

***Corn Sauté***

| | | |
|---|---|---|
| 4 Tbsp | unsalted butter | 50 mL |
| 1 cup | finely chopped red onion | 250 mL |
| 1 cup | diced zucchini | 250 mL |
| 2 cups | fresh corn kernels (2 large cobs) | 500 mL |

***Tomato–Basil Relish***

| | | |
|---|---|---|
| 8 | fresh plum tomatoes, peeled, seeded and diced | 8 |
| ½ tsp | salt | 2 mL |
| 1 | small, fresh hot cherry pepper, roasted, peeled, seeded and diced | 1 |
| 12 | large basil leaves, cut crosswise into thin strips | 12 |
| | basil sprigs for garnish | |

### *Relish*

• Mix the diced tomatoes and ½ tsp/2 mL salt. Place in a sieve and let drain for an hour. Mix with the cherry pepper and set aside.

• Preheat the grill.

### *Corn Sauté*

• In a large pan, melt the butter over medium heat. Add the red onion and sauté until the onion becomes translucent. Add the zucchini and sauté just until it starts to become translucent. Stir in the corn and sauté for another 4–5 minutes, until everything is piping hot. Remove from the heat and keep warm.

• Mix the basil in with tomato mixture.

• Sprinkle the salmon with the salt and pepper. Grill the salmon skin side up for 3–4 minutes. Turn over and grill for another 3–4 minutes until the salmon is cooked but still juicy on the inside. Remove from the grill.

• Spoon the corn onto 4 heated plates. Place the salmon on top of the corn and spoon the tomato relish on top of the salmon. Garnish with sprigs of basil.

*The cleanest, freshest-tasting trout I have ever eaten are farmed by Mike Phillips, an outdoorsman and naturalist whose knowlege of the out-of-doors was inspired by a thirty-day survival test in the army years ago. A totally secluded, extra-cold (43.1°F) water source lies on his Walters Falls, Ontario property, high up on the Niagara escarpment. This super-clean, extra-cold water, says Mike, is the key to the high quality and health of his fish.*

*Phillips has personally tested his water for 2,800 chemicals, and found none of them. (He says ordinary drinking water contains 1,800.) His fish are fed O.C.I.A.-certified organic feed and, he claims, are raised under the strictest of conditions — so strict that his emissions are cleaner than the water used by most fish farms that are currently licensed by the Ministry of Natural Resources.*

*To make this recipe, Chef Kenneth Peace saves up the discarded stems from herbs he has used in the kitchen (thyme, rosemary, basil, oregano, etc.) It's easy for you to do this at home, too — just collect them in a plastic bag in your crisper. When you've accumulated 4 oz/125 g, spread them on a baking sheet and dry in a warm oven, and you're ready to proceed.*

# Herb-Smoked Trout with Yogurt and Caper Dressing

KENNETH PEACE
O'Keefe Centre
*Toronto, Ontario*

SERVES 4

**Trout**

| | | |
|---|---|---|
| 1 lb | boneless trout fillets | 454 g |
| 4 oz | dried herb stems | 125 g |
| pinch | salt | pinch |
| pinch | white pepper | pinch |
| pinch | sugar | pinch |

### *Dressing*

| | | |
|---|---|---|
| 2 Tbsp | chopped shallots | 25 mL |
| 2 Tbsp | chopped red pepper | 25 mL |
| 1 Tbsp | olive oil | 15 mL |
| ¾ cup | yogurt, drained in cheesecloth | 175 mL |
| ¼ cup | chopped capers | 50 mL |
| 2 tsp | red peppercorns, chopped or cracked if dry | 10 mL |
| ¼ cup | fresh dill, chopped | 50 mL |
| 2 Tbsp | lemon juice | 25 mL |
| 3 Tbsp | balsamic vinegar | 50 mL |
| 1 tsp | dijon mustard | 5 mL |
| 4 | handfuls mixed baby salad greens and seedlings | 4 |
| | cucumber slices and roasted mustard seeds for garnish | |

• Sauté shallots and red pepper in olive oil over low heat until shallots are transparent. Set aside to cool. Combine with other dressing ingredients, season to taste and refrigerate for at least 1 hour.
• Soak herb stems in water for 15 minutes, drain, then place in a dry, very hot skillet (preferably cast iron).
• Place trout fillets, skin side down, on top of the herb stems. Season with salt, pepper and sugar. Cover with lid and smoke for approximately 10 minutes or until trout flesh is just cooked.
• Remove trout, break into shards without skin, and place on top of greens and seedlings. Finish with dressing. Garnish with cucumber slices sprinkled with roasted mustard seeds.

Trout fillets may be obtained from Highland Springs Trout Farm, Walters Falls, Ontario. Trout is also sold at the Knives and Forks Market, The Big Carrot and selected health food retailers throughout Ontario. *(See Source Information at back of book.)*

# Oven-Baked, Herb-Crusted Monkfish with a Tomato–Basil Salsa

KURT WALDELE
Le Café, National Arts Centre
*Ottawa, Ontario*

SERVES 4

***Fish***

| | | |
|---|---|---|
| 12 | ½-inch/1.5-cm slices of monkfish, skinless and boneless (approximately 2 oz/60 g each) | 12 |
| 1 Tbsp | olive oil | 15 mL |

***Crust***

| | | |
|---|---|---|
| 6 | slices white bread, crusts removed | 6 |
| ¼ cup | extra-virgin oil | 50 mL |
| 1 Tbsp | each: finely chopped fresh italian parsley and dill | 15 mL |
| 1 tsp | chopped fresh cilantro | 5 mL |
| 2 | shallots, finely chopped | 2 |
| 1 | clove garlic, finely chopped | 1 |

***Tomato–Basil Salsa***

| | | |
|---|---|---|
| 2 | medum-sized, ripe tomatoes | 2 |
| 2 Tbsp | chopped fresh basil leaves | 25 mL |
| 1 | shallot, finely chopped | 1 |
| 1 | clove garlic, finely chopped | 1 |
| 1 Tbsp | extra-virgin olive oil | 15 mL |
| 2 Tbsp | balsamic vinegar | 25 mL |
| ¼ | fresh jalapeño, seeds removed, finely chopped | ¼ |
| | salt and freshly ground black pepper | |

*Tomato–Basil Salsa*

• Remove core from the tomatoes and make a cross-shaped incision on the opposite side. Blanch tomatoes in boiling water for approximately 1 minute or until skins loosen slightly.

• Transfer tomatoes to a bowl of ice water, cool and peel. Cut tomato into quarters and remove the seeds. Cut into fine cubes. In a glass or porcelain bowl, combine tomatoes with remaining ingredients. Cover and refrigerate overnight before serving, to allow the flavours to blend.

• Place white bread in a food processor and process until reduced to crumbs. Add olive oil, parsley, dill, cilantro, shallots and garlic and mix well.

• Preheat oven to 425°F/220°C. Season fish with salt and pepper. Rub fish with olive oil and place in a baking pan. Top with the bread crumb mixture. Pat down mixture lightly. Bake in a hot oven until bread crumbs are golden and crusty (approximately 5–7 minutes).

• Remove fish from the pan and place on warmed plates. Serve with tomato–basil salsa and your favourite vegetables and potatoes.

*One of the first differences Susan Weaver noticed between cooking in Canada and the U.S. after her arrival in Toronto from Houston in 1989 was "the strong emphasis here on fresh produce." In the kitchen of The Four Seasons Hotel trays of fresh herbs and seedlings still in soil line the walls, to be snipped at just the right moment.*

*Weaver became affiliated with Knives and Forks as part of an ongoing effort to find the best quality ingredients available from local suppliers. To help her associates in the kitchen develop an appreciation for the origin of various ingredients, she established a pilot program whereby cooks and apprentices spend time at Cookstown Greens during harvesting and planting seasons.*

*This unique method for curing salmon developed by Susan Weaver is a mainstay on the hotel's menu. It makes a fabulous hors d'oeuvre.*

# Pastrami Salmon

SUSAN WEAVER
The Four Seasons Hotel
*Toronto, Ontario*

SERVES 10–12

| | | |
|---|---|---|
| 1 | side fresh salmon, boneless and with skin (approximately 3 lbs/1.4 kg) | 1 |

***Marinade***

| | | |
|---|---|---|
| 2¼ cups | kosher salt | 550 mL |
| ½ cup | granulated sugar | 125 mL |
| 2 Tbsp | vegetable oil | 25 mL |

***Salmon Topping***

| | | |
|---|---|---|
| 3 Tbsp | black peppercorn, crushed | 50 mL |
| 3 Tbsp | coriander seeds, crushed | 50 mL |
| 1 Tbsp | brown sugar | 15 mL |
| pinch | ground allspice | pinch |
| pinch | ground cloves | pinch |

• Begin by laying salmon, skin side down, on a flat tray or baking sheet.
• Combine marinade ingredients and distribute entire mixture across the top of the salmon, using less at the tail and thinner side of the salmon. Cover with plastic wrap and refrigerate for 24 hours.
• Remove salmon from refrigerator and rinse thoroughly with cold water. Pat dry with paper towels. Place on a clean platter, skin side down. Salmon must now be dried. Place an electric fan blowing on the salmon at room temperature for 4 hours.
• Combine topping ingredients and distribute evenly across the salmon, lightly pressing mixture into the fish.
• Slice salmon thinly and serve on your favourite bread. Try it with assorted mustards, pickles and cold beer. Salmon will keep for at least 10 days in the refrigerator, covered loosely with waxed paper.

*Torontonians may well remember Alan Groom as the chef who introduced them to* cuisine minceur *at Chives in the 1970s. His innovative seasonal cooking at L'Hardy's some ten years later brought praise from Joanne Kates. Then came a brief return to England and his own dining room, from which he was hired by Charles Khabouth to run Oceans, where his fanciful and exciting dishes drew rave reviews. After briefly heading up Oceans' reincarnation as the Ivory Lounge, Groom moved to Vancouver in 1991.*

*At Bacchus, the Wedgewood Hotel's Italian restaurant, Groom serves what may be the best-tasting fish in town. His secret? "Get it fresh, cook it simply and sell it fast."*

# Plum-Glazed Wild Salmon with Sorrel Sauce, Pea-tops and Redcurrant Salad

ALAN GROOM
Bacchus Restaurant at the Wedgewood Hotel
*Vancouver, British Columbia*

SERVES 4

***Plum Glaze***

| | | |
|---|---|---|
| 1 lb | ripe plums, peeled, halved and pitted | 454 g |
| ½ cup | sugar | 125 mL |
| 1 | fresh ginger, 1-inch/2.5-cm piece, finely chopped | 1 |
| 1 | small chili pepper, seeded and finely chopped | 1 |

| | | |
|---|---|---|
| 2 lbs | salmon fillets | 1 kg |
| 6 oz | fresh sorrel, leaves only, washed and chopped | 175 g |
| ½ cup | unsalted butter | 125 mL |
| 1 Tbsp | chopped shallots | 15 mL |

| | | |
|---|---|---|
| ¼ cup | white wine | 50 mL |
| | juice of 1 lemon | |
| 1 lb | pea-tops (the delicately flavoured upper shoot of the shelling pea or sugar snap pea), washed | 454 g |
| ½ lb | red currants, picked over | 225 g |

### *Plum glaze*

• Pre-heat oven to 400°F/200°C.

• Heat plums, sugar, ginger and chili in a saucepan over medium heat until sugar caramelizes. Add 1 cup/250 mL water and reduce until it becomes a glaze. Strain.

### *Sauce*

• Bring wine, shallots and lemon juice to a boil. Simmer until reduced to a spoonful. Add sorrel, reduce heat, adding butter piece by piece, whisking in gradually. Remove from heat.

### *Pea-top Salad*

• Dress pea-tops with a light vinaigrette dressing and garnish with red currants.

• Brush salmon with glaze and place in oven or under a broiler for approximately 5 minutes, until medium-rare.

### *Presentation*

• Pour sauce on plates and top with glazed salmon fillets. Serve with the pea-top salad.

The restaurant obtains pea-tops, sorrel and currants from Glorious Garnishes. *(See Source Information at back of book.)*

*Organics is a thirty-four seat bistro in downtown Toronto. Chef John Christou, who has been with the restaurant since it opened in December of 1991, has been an advocate of organic food for a long time, and endeavours to use as much as possible.*

*Health and environmental concerns influence several aspects of the restaurant's operation: from offering a selection of organic wines, to cooking with filtered water and using toxin-free utensils (stainless steel, wood or glass; not plastic and aluminum).*

# Poached Pike Fillets with Wild Leeks, Fiddleheads and Jerusalem Artichokes

JOHN CHRISTOU
Organics Restaurant
*Toronto, Ontario*

SERVES 6

| | | |
|---|---|---|
| 1½ lbs | jerusalem artichokes | 750 g |
| | juice from 1 lemon | |
| 2 quarts | spring water | 2L |
| | sea salt | |
| 2 cups | fiddleheads | 500 mL |
| 12 bunches | wild leeks, julienned | 12 bunches |
| 6 | pike fillets, 6 oz/175 g each | 6 |
| ¼ cup | safflower oil | 50 mL |
| ½ tsp | chopped fresh garlic | 2 mL |
| | salt and pepper | |
| 1 Tbsp | chive flower vinegar | 15 mL |
| 2 Tbsp | butter | 25 mL |
| ½ cup | white wine | 125 mL |

***Court Bouillon***

| | | |
|---|---|---|
| 3 cups | spring water | 750 mL |
| ¼ cup | white wine (preferably organic) | 50 mL |

| | | |
|---|---|---|
| 1 | stalk celery | 1 |
| 1 | leek | 1 |
| 1 | bay leaf | 1 |
| 1 | clove | 1 |
| pinch | each: tarragon, parsley, chervil | pinch |
| 8 | white peppercorns | 8 |
| ½ | lemon, sliced | ½ |
| 1 | sprig coriander | 1 |

***Chive Flower Vinegar***

| | | |
|---|---|---|
| ⅔ cup | plain vinegar | 150 mL |
| ¼ cup | white wine | 50 mL |
| 8 | chive flowers | 8 |

• Clean and peel artichokes and slice in ⅛-inch/3-mm thicknesses. Cover with cold water and the lemon juice to prevent oxidation.

• Boil 2 quarts/2 L of spring water and the sea salt. Blanch the jerusalem artichokes in boiling water for 1½ minutes. Refresh in cold water. Drain.

• Bring all ingredients for the court bouillon to a simmer in a large pot or fish poacher. Poach fillets in the bouillon for 7–8 minutes or until just done. Remove from heat. Remove fillets from the liquid and keep warm; reserve liquid.

• Boil the fiddleheads in a large kettle of boiling water over high heat for 3 minutes. Drain. Refresh in cold water to stop cooking. **Do not overcook.**

• Sauté artichokes in safflower oil and garlic. Deglaze with ¼ cup/50 mL of strained court bouillon. Add chive flower vinegar and salt and pepper to taste.

• Sauté wild leeks in butter; deglaze with ½ cup/125 mL white wine and reduce by half.

• To serve, place a pike fillet on each plate. Top with some of the sautéed leeks, and serve with the steamed fiddleheads and the jerusalem artichokes.

***Chive Flower Vinegar***

• Combine all ingredients in a bowl, then pour into a glass bottle. Seal and allow to infuse for 1 week.

*Passionate about haute cuisine, Claude Postel's approach to cooking over the years has evolved into a style that pleases the eye as well as the palate.*

*His restaurant and namesake is one of the best in Montréal in the French tradition, and is perhaps best known for its famed seven course "menu gastronomique." Situated in a charming, fully restored 19th-century house, the restaurant has been open since 1989.*

# Salmon Scallops Claude Postel

CLAUDE POSTEL
Claude Postel
*Montréal, Québec*

SERVES 4

| | | |
|---|---|---|
| 4 | slices fresh salmon fillets (preferably Atlantic), 2 oz/60 g each | 4 |
| 4 | slices smoked salmon | 4 |
| 4 | shallots, peeled | 4 |
| 5 Tbsp | sherry | 70 mL |
| 5 Tbsp | sweet butter | 70 mL |
| ¼ cup | 35% cream | 50 mL |
| | juice of ½ lemon | |
| pinch | salt and freshly ground black pepper | pinch |
| 2 Tbsp | finely chopped parsley | 25 mL |

• Bring the 4 shallots to a boil in the sherry, and then simmer until completely reduced. Add the 35% cream and the butter in small pieces and a pinch of salt and pepper. Reduce over high heat, making sure not to burn the sides of the saucepan. Stir in the lemon juice. Keep warm.

• Top each salmon fillet with a slice of smoked salmon. Cook in a lightly buttered skillet over high heat, covered, for 3 minutes.

• Pour the thoroughly warmed sauce over 4 large, warm plates. When the first slice of salmon appears light pink, it is done. Place it immediately on the sauce. Sprinkle with chopped parsley. Serve immediately.

*Tucked away in a comfortable country house in the town of Cap-Chat, in the Gaspé, is one of that region's best restaurants, Le Cabillaud. Yvan Belzile, who has served as its executive chef since 1982, is self-trained and is always in search of new recipes from near and far.*

*A lover of nature as well as cooking, Belzile grows all of his herbs, vegetables and fruits organically, smokes his own salmon, and makes fresh bread every day. Although the restaurant is only open from mid-June to mid-September, it makes the most of its location and features many varieties of fresh-caught local fish and seafood.*

*A beautiful view of the Gulf of the St. Lawrence makes Le Cabillaud an ideal place to savour the treasures of the North Atlantic.*

# Scallop Mousse with Beurre Blanc

YVAN BELZILE
Le Cabillaud
*Cap-Chat Est, Québec*

SERVES 6

| | | |
|---|---|---|
| ½ lb | scallops | 225 g |
| 3 oz | fillet of sole | 90 g |
| 1 | large egg white | 1 |
| | salt and pepper | |
| 1 cup | 35% cream | 250 mL |

***Beurre Blanc***

| | | |
|---|---|---|
| ¼ cup | white table wine | 50 mL |
| ¼ cup | white wine vinegar | 50 mL |
| 2 Tbsp | 35% cream | 25 mL |
| ½ cup | very cold butter | 125 mL |

• In a food processor purée the sole and the scallops. Transfer to a bowl and, by hand, mix in the egg white, the salt and pepper, then add 1/4 cup/50 mL of the cream. Combine well and refrigerate for half an hour.
• Add another 1/4 cup/50 mL of cream and return to the refrigerator for another half hour.
• Whip the remaining 1/2 cup/125 mL of cream and fold in carefully with a spatula.
• Butter 6 ramekins and place a small circle of waxed paper in the bottom of each. Spoon in the mousse and cover with aluminum foil.
• Fill a rectangular baking dish, large enough to accommodate the six ramekins, halfway with boiling water and cook in a 350°F/180°C for 15 minutes or until the mousse has set. Do not overcook or it will separate. Keep warm.

### *Beurre Blanc*

• In a small saucepan, reduce the wine and the vinegar by half. Add the cream and reduce until glossy. Reduce the heat and whisk in the butter in large pieces until the butter is completely melted. This sauce should be made at the last minute and should not boil.

Unmold each mousse and set in the centre of a hot plate. Encircle with the beurre blanc, and garnish with a cooked shrimp and a leaf of italian parsley.

The mousse reheats well in an oven if the dish has become chilled.

# Oysters in Nasturtium Flower Butter

SINCLAIR PHILIP
Sooke Harbour House
*Sooke, British Columbia*

SERVES 4

| | | |
|---|---|---|
| 2½ cups | fish stock | 625 mL |
| ½ cup | dry white wine | 125 mL |
| 1 Tbsp | nasturtium flower vinegar (or substitute white wine vinegar) | 15 mL |
| 8 | large nasturtium leaves, minced | 8 |
| 16 | nasturtium flowers, coarsely chopped (preferably a variety of colours) | 16 |
| 1½ cups | unsalted butter | 375 mL |
| 16 | large oysters, shucked | 16 |
| | nasturtium blossoms and leaves for garnish | |

• You will need two sauté pans, one for sauce, another in which to grill oysters. In the first pan, combine stock, wine and vinegar. Place over high heat and bring to a boil. Continue to cook uncovered, until liquid is reduced to about ½ cup/125 mL. Remove from heat and stir in nasturtium leaves and flowers. Whisk in butter, a spoonful at a time, to create a smooth sauce.

• While liquids are reducing, heat second skillet over medium-high heat, brushing it with a little vegetable oil. Grill oysters quickly on both sides until golden around edges. Keep oysters warm while you finish the sauce.

• Spoon sauce onto 4 heated plates. Place 4 oysters on each plate and garnish with small nasturtium leaves and 3 or 4 nasturtium flowers. This dish is wonderful with crusty whole wheat bread and a crisp white wine, such as chardonnay.

# POULTRY

*Wrex Roth knows a lot about chickens. The Prince Edward County, Ontario farmer has been raising them since 1975. In the mid-1980s he began to feed his birds various types of grains to see if it made any difference in the flavour of the chickens. He discovered that birds that had been fed organically grown grain tasted far superior to the chickens that were not.*

*"How you raise them and what you feed them are the two biggest factors that affect their flavour," he says. To the best of Roth's knowledge, his Roth Family Farms in Picton, Ontario is the only certified organic chicken producer in Canada, shipping 2,500 chickens per week, no small operation by any means.*

*Several significant factors distinguish organically raised chickens from their mass-produced counterparts. In most poultry farms birds are confined to cages allotting between .75 and .85 square foot per bird, while Roth's chickens have more than four times as much open space per bird (about four square feet) to run around in. However, Roth emphasizes that his chickens are not free range. "There are a lot of misconceptions about what makes a chicken free range. A lot of people assume that it merely means not confined to cages. In actuality it means that the chickens are running around* outside. *In Canada, you simply cannot raise chickens outdoors in most climates, so the term is somewhat misused. Free range also gives no indication of what may have been administered to the chickens during their development. (In this book, the term free range implies that the poultry has been raised without chemicals, fed whole grains, and raised under humane conditions.)*

*Roth's chickens take approximately seven-and-a-half to eight weeks to mature, versus six weeks for conventionally raised birds. Although he won't point any fingers, Roth suspects that those chickens must be receiving some synthetic substances to further accelerate their development.*

*Willy Fida is fortunate his restaurant is only a few miles from Roth's farm. Fida obtains chickens from Roth year round.*

# Chicken with Fresh Basil and Black Olives

WILLY FIDA
Angeline's Restaurants
*Bloomfield, Ontario*

SERVES 4

| | | |
|---|---|---|
| 2–2½ lbs | organic chicken | 1 kg |
| | salt and pepper | |
| 1 tsp | peanut oil | 5 mL |

***Sauce***

| | | |
|---|---|---|
| 1 tsp | butter | 5 mL |
| 1 | chopped shallot | 1 |
| ¼ cup | dry white wine | 50 mL |
| 6 Tbsp | clear chicken stock | 100 mL |
| ½ cup | 35% cream | 125 mL |
| 2 Tbsp | pesto (recipe follows) | 25 mL |
| 1 Tbsp | butter | 15 mL |
| | salt and pepper | |
| few drops | lemon juice | few drops |
| 3 | black olives, cut in strips | 3 |
| 1 Tbsp | freshly cut chives | 15 mL |
| 1 | tomato, diced | 1 |

***Pesto***

*Purée together in a blender or food processor*

| | | |
|---|---|---|
| 5–6 | fresh basil leaves | 5–6 |
| 3 Tbsp | olive oil | 50 mL |
| 1 | clove garlic | 1 |

• Preheat oven to 350°F/180°C. Disjoint chicken by taking off both breasts and removing legs. Separate leg from thigh.

• Season chicken with salt and pepper. Heat oil in a large skillet and sauté chicken on both sides until golden brown. Remove to a roasting pan and roast in the oven for 45 minutes or until done.

### *Sauce*

• Melt butter over medium heat in a saucepan. Add chopped shallots and sauté until transparent. Deglaze with white wine. Reduce by one half. Add chicken stock and bring to a boil. Simmer until reduced by half. Stir in the 35% cream and simmer gently without boiling until thickened.
• Add pesto to finished sauce, seasoning with salt and pepper and lemon juice to taste. Finish sauce by adding a julienne of black olives.
• Place roasted chicken pieces on dinner plate. Top with sauce and garnish with diced tomatoes and freshly cut chives.

Roth Chickens are available at the Knives and Forks Market, Noah's Natural Foods, and The Big Carrot, all in Toronto. (*See Source Information at back of book.*)

*Calgary-born and raised, Paul Rogalski's cooking remains true to his prairie roots. "In this area we specialize in things like meat, duck, game and local wild fish," he says enthusiastically. In homage to the local bounty, every fall La Chaumière holds Celebrate the Seasons, an annual game festival, where such items as boar, raised especially for the restaurant, and their famous Cinnamon-Smoked Breast of Pheasant are featured. This recipe is superb as is, or, if you wish, add a couple of cinnamon sticks to the birchwood chips for a pungent, earthy taste.*

# Birch-Smoked Prairie Pheasant with Wild Berry Chutney

PAUL ROGALSKI
La Chaumière
*Calgary, Alberta*

SERVES 4–6

| | | |
|---|---|---|
| 2 oz | birchwood chips | 60 g |
| 6 | pheasant breasts | 6 |
| | salt and pepper | |
| | olive oil | |

***Wild Berry Chutney***

| | | |
|---|---|---|
| ¼ cup | wild blueberries | 50 mL |
| ¼ cup | saskatoon berries | 50 mL |
| ¼ cup | fresh raspberries | 50 mL |
| ¼ cup | field strawberries | 50 mL |
| ¼ cup | white wine vinegar | 50 mL |
| 1 tsp | chopped fresh thyme | 5 mL |
| 1 | bay leaf | 1 |
| 1 tsp | cracked black pepper | 5 mL |
| | sugar | |

• Combine all the ingredients for the chutney except sugar in a sauce pan and bring to a simmer. Cook for 15 minutes, stirring occasionally. Remove from heat and let cool at room temperature. Add sugar to taste.

• Place birchwood chips in an old metal pie plate and moisten slightly with water.

• Preheat charcoal or gas barbecue.

• Set the pie plate directly on the coals and wait for the wood to smoulder. Once it has reached this stage, reduce heat or adjust the grill to a cooler position.

• Season the pheasant with salt and pepper and brush with olive oil. Place on the barbecue grill and close the lid. Cook for 10 minutes or until the meat is firm to the touch. Remove from heat and let stand for 5 minutes.

• Thinly slice the pheasant breasts and serve with the wild berry chutney.

*Food is centre stage at Auberge Hatley, one of this country's most elegant country inns and a member of the prestigious Relais & Châteaux, an international group of fine hotels. With its warm, inviting atmosphere, historic environs, splendid facilities and breathtaking view of Lake Massawippi, in Quebec's Eastern Townships, Auberge Hatley has much to draw the well-heeled traveller to its doors. But it is the food that makes visitors happy to return.*

*Chef Alain Labrie trained at L'institut de Tourisme et de l'Hôtellerie du Québec in Fort Préval, Gaspé, and has perfected his art in some of the finest restaurants in the province. He was named chef just six months after he arrived at the inn in April, 1989.*

*When I first contacted Labrie, he said he would be delighted to contribute a recipe to my book, and casually mentioned that the Auberge had its own greenhouse. What I did not know was that "greenhouse" actually meant an 8,500 square foot plastic and steel environment that supplies the inn, along with many of the area's other restaurants, with exotic lettuces, herbs and edible flowers, all of which are grown hydroponically. (The hydroponic method entails growing on raised soil-less beds in a strictly-controlled environment. The plants are also irrigated with a dissolved nutrient solution. Although no pesticides or herbicides are used, by definition the plants are not considered to be organic.) The greenhouse, however, does provide the restaurant with wonderful fresh greens in an area of the country where the growing season is quite short, and often inspires Labrie to create new recipes, such as this flavourful chicken dish.*

# Casserole of Grain-Fed Chicken with Fresh Herbs and Balsamic Vinegar

ALAIN LABRIE
Auberge Hatley
*North Hatley, Québec*

SERVES 6

| | | |
|---|---|---|
| 6 lb | grain fed chicken | 3 kg |
| ½ cup | extra-virgin olive oil | 125 mL |
| 5 Tbsp | balsamic vinegar | 70 mL |
| 2 Tbsp | chopped fresh basil | 25 mL |
| 2 Tbsp | chopped fresh thyme | 25 mL |
| 2 Tbsp | chopped fresh chervil | 25 mL |
| 2 Tbsp | chopped fresh rosemary | 25 mL |
| 1 | clove garlic, peeled and chopped | 1 |
| ½ cup | red wine | 125 mL |
| 2 cups | chicken stock | 500 mL |
| 2 Tbsp | tamari (soy sauce) | 25 mL |
| 1 tsp | butter | 5 mL |
| 1 tsp | flour | 5 mL |

• Cut the chicken into 12 pieces and combine with the olive oil, balsamic vinegar, basil, thyme, chervil, rosemary and garlic. Marinate in the refrigerator for 24 hours.

• Remove the chicken and set in a casserole with a cover. Pour the red wine over the chicken. Add the chicken stock, the remaining marinade and the tamari.

• Cook, covered, in a preheated 375°F/190°C oven for 45 minutes until done. Remove the chicken from the roasting pan.

• Heat the butter in a saucepan and stir in the flour with a whisk. Cook for a minute then add all the liquid from the roasting pan. Bring to a boil, then simmer, whisking occasionally, until slightly thickened. Pour over the chicken and serve.

# Chicken Breast Stuffed with Wild Rice and Mushrooms

RICK MADDISON
Capers
*Vancouver, British Columbia*

SERVES 4

| | | |
|---|---|---|
| 4 | boneless chicken breasts, skinned | 4 |
| 4 oz | shiitake mushrooms | 125 g |
| | salt and pepper | |
| 2 Tbsp | butter | 25 mL |
| 3 Tbsp | shallots, finely chopped | 50 mL |
| 2 | cloves garlic, chopped | 2 |
| ¾ cup | cooked wild rice | 175 mL |
| 2 Tbsp | chopped fresh sage | 25 mL |
| ¼ cup | white wine or heavy cream (optional) | 50 mL |

• Remove the tenderloins from the underside of the chicken breasts and chop finely. Set aside.
• Clean the shiitake mushrooms thoroughly. Remove and discard the stems. Coarsely chop the tops.
• Preheat oven to 350°F/180°C. Pound chicken breasts with a mallet until ⅜ inch/1 cm thick. Sprinkle both sides of breast with salt and pepper.
• Melt butter in saucepan and cook shallots, slowly, for 2 minutes. Add shiitake mushrooms, finely chopped tenderloin, and garlic. Cook for about 10 minutes until all moisture has evaporated from mushrooms.
• Remove from heat and transfer to a bowl along with the cooked wild rice and sage. Add a pinch of salt and pepper and mix well. Spoon ¼ of the mixture on the underside of each breast. Fold breast over and secure with toothpicks or twine.

• Preheat a cast iron or non-stick frying pan on medium heat. Cook breast on each side for 3–4 minutes, then place in oven for an additional 10 minutes. Remove from pan and place breasts on individual plates.

• If desired, return frying pan to heat and add ¼ cup/50 mL of wine or heavy cream. Stir briefly and pour sauce over chicken.

*English-born Martin Ritins offers North York high school students a smattering of environmental awareness along with their daily lunch. As the owner of Martin's Catering, he is responsible for serving lunch to seventy-five hungry students each day. Their appreciation of the links between food, personal health and the health of the land began by instituting a recycling and composting program in the school; a visit to Rowe Farms in Guelph offered insights into how a farm is managed.*

*Chef Alli Millar, whose experience includes eighteen years in restaurants in Toronto, New York and Stratford, Ontario found feeding high school students "with a McDonald's background" presented an unusual challenge; in her words, "just getting them to eat vegetables was an accomplishment."*

# Crispy Roast Chicken with Pasta in Roasted Yellow Tomato Sauce

ALLI MILLAR
Martin's Catering
*North York, Ontario*

SERVES 4

| | | |
|---|---|---|
| 4 | large, very ripe yellow tomatoes, cored | 4 |
| 1 | yellow onion | 1 |
| ½ | head garlic, in one piece | ½ |
| 3 | sprigs fresh thyme (leaves only) | 3 |
| ¼ cup | olive oil | 50 mL |
| 1 cup | hearty red wine | 250 mL |
| 3 | sprigs fresh oregano (leaves only) | 3 |
| 1 | good-sized bunch fresh basil | 1 |
| 1 Tbsp | balsamic vinegar | 15 mL |
| | sea salt and pepper | |

| | | |
|---|---|---|
| 12 oz | dried spaghetti or spaghettini | 350 g |
| 2 | whole chicken breasts, split, with skin | 2 |
| ¼ cup | olive oil | 50 mL |
| 12 | fresh basil leaves | 12 |

- Preheat oven to 350°F/180°C.
- Place tomatoes, onion and garlic (with skins still on) in a roasting pan. Lay thyme on onion and tomato. Sprinkle with sea salt and pepper. Drizzle with olive oil. Roast in oven approximately 1 hour until onion and garlic are very soft and tomatoes are nearly charred. Remove garlic and onion, but leave tomato in the oven while you complete the next step. Slit onion skin and squeeze out soft pulp into a small bowl. Repeat with garlic.
- Heat a heavy skillet and add ¼ cup/50 mL olive oil. Add onion and garlic and stir briskly. Add red wine and reduce by one quarter. Add tomatoes and all of the pan juices and continue to cook over high heat, stirring constantly.
- Add basil and oregano and season with sea salt, balsamic vinegar and freshly-ground black pepper to taste.
- Raise oven to 375°F/190°C.
- Trim chicken breasts and tuck 3 basil leaves under the skin of each breast.
- Bring a large kettle of salted water to a full rolling boil and lower heat slightly while you begin to prepare the chicken.
- Heat olive oil in a heavy, ovenproof skillet and place chicken, skin side down, in the pan. Season with sea salt and pepper. When the skin has turned golden brown, turn.
- Turn chicken once more to skin side down and place skillet in oven.
- Bring the water back to a boil and add the pasta.
- Stir pasta. Chicken will be done when the pasta is *al dente*.
- Drain pasta and toss with the sauce.
- Slice chicken and arrange on plate over pasta.

Yellow and orange tomatoes are available in season from Cookstown Greens and Burgess and Martin Organic Farms. *(See Source Information at back of book.)*

*Serge Bruyère cooked with Paul Bocuse, Jacques Le Divillec and the Troisgros brothers, then spent three years at L'Auberge du Tunnel in Auvergne in his native France before coming to Canada in 1976 to cook at the Olympics. In 1980 he opened his own restaurant, which offers three different tiers of service in a resplendent old building in the heart of Québec City.*

*As the first chef in Québec to introduce "la nouvelle cuisine Québécoise," a style of cooking that emphasizes regional and organically-grown ingredients, Bruyère obtains a good deal of the restaurant's vegetables from local farmers on the Ile d'Orléans. Finding organic produce aesthetically more pleasing, as well as being more flavourful, Bruyère also claims that it is cleaner than other produce he has worked with. This saves time and effort in the kitchen because "we don't have to wash it as much." However, he emphasizes, "We are not fanatics. Organic products are not always available, and out of season they are very expensive. Our philosophy is to use what is fresh."*

*In the winter, that may mean transforming a humble chicken and a head of cabbage from the cellar into a dish that satisfies both palate and soul.*

# Farmer's Chicken with Buttered Cabbage

SERGE BRUYÈRE
À la Table de Serge Bruyère
*Québec City, Québec*

SERVES 4

| | | |
|---|---|---|
| 3 lb | grain-fed chicken | 1.5 kg |
| 1 | head of green cabbage | 1 |
| 1 lb | slab of smoked bacon | 454 g |
| 2 | yellow cooking onions | 2 |
| 1 | carrot | 1 |

| | | |
|---|---|---|
| ½ cup | butter | 125 mL |
| 2 | cloves garlic | 2 |
| | salt and pepper | |

### *Chicken*

• Preheat the oven to 375°F/190°C. Prepare the chicken for roasting: cut off the neck and the wingtips, then tie with twine. Season the interior cavity with salt and pepper, then place two whole, unpeeled cloves of garlic inside. Place the chicken on a roasting pan, surrounded by the giblets and 1 Tbsp/15 mL of butter.

• Roast for 30 minutes, then add one onion and the carrot, cut into pieces. Return to the oven for an additional 30 minutes. When cooked, remove the chicken and keep warm.

• Pour off the pan juices into a saucepan and add 1 cup/250 mL of water. Simmer for 20 minutes over medium heat. Add salt and pepper to taste.

### *Cabbage*

• Remove the outer leaves of the cabbage. Cut into quarters. Remove the centre core. Shred coarsely.

• Cut the smoked bacon into strips and place in a saucepan, with cold water to cover. Bring to a boil. Remove with a slotted spoon, drain, and refresh under cold water.

• Heat 1 Tbsp/15 mL butter in a saucepan over medium heat. Add the chopped onion and toss until transparent.

• Add the bacon and shredded cabbage. Cook to meld flavours, then add ½ cup/125 mL of water. Cover and let simmer for about 10 minutes. When the cabbage is nearly done, add the remaining 2 Tbsp/25 mL of butter to thicken.

Place the buttered cabbage on 4 plates, along with half a breast and half a leg for each person. Spoon the sauce over and serve warm.

# Free Range Chicken with a Lemon Preserve

LOUIS GERVAIS
Le Club at Le Meridien
*Vancouver, British Columbia*

SERVES 6

| | | |
|---|---|---|
| 3 | boneless chicken breasts, halved and skinned | 3 |
| 1 oz | kalamata olives, pitted and chopped | 30 g |
| 3 Tbsp | unsalted butter | 50 mL |
| 1 Tbsp | fresh lemon juice | 15 mL |
| 2 Tbsp | julienned lemon zest | 25 mL |
| 2 Tbsp | sugar | 25 mL |
| 1 Tbsp | minced shallots | 15 mL |
| 4½ cups | chicken stock | 1.13 L |
| 24 | small new potatoes, scrubbed | 24 |

***Baby organic vegetables***

| | | |
|---|---|---|
| 12 | zucchini | 12 |
| 12 | carrots | 12 |
| 12 | beets | 12 |
| 1 | head red kale, julienned | 1 |

• Put the sugar in a small, heavy-bottomed pan and swirl it over very low heat without stirring; it will slowly melt and turn golden. Make a "gastric" by deglazing the caramelized sugar with the lemon juice.

• In another pan, sweat the lemon zest, olives and shallots in 1 Tbsp/15 mL of the butter. Add to the gastric.

• Add chicken stock to the mixture. Bring to a boil, then simmer until thickened and finish with butter.

- Sauté the potatoes in 1 Tbsp/15 mL butter, then transfer buttered potatoes to a preheated 375°F/190°C oven for 20 minutes to finish cooking.
- Pan fry the chicken breasts.
- Meanwhile, steam zucchini, carrots and beets.
- Pan fry the kale in the remaining 1 Tbsp/15 mL of butter, deglazing with a splash or two of water, if necessary.
- Slice chicken breast and place in the middle of plate. Decorate with 3 potatoes, the baby vegetables and kale. Top with the sauce.

# Free Range Turkey Breast with Summer Fruit and Southern Comfort

GLEN VAN BLOMMESTEIM
Overtures
*Tecumseh, Ontario*

SERVES 6

| | | |
|---|---|---|
| 6 | slices free range turkey breast | 6 |
| | salt and pepper | |
| ½ cup | dijon mustard | 125 mL |
| 2 cups | ground pecans | 500 mL |
| ¼ cup | safflower oil | 50 mL |

***Summer Fruit Compote***

| | | |
|---|---|---|
| ¼ cup | alfalfa honey | 50 mL |
| | juice from 1 lemon | |
| 9 | fresh apricots, washed, pitted and quartered | 9 |
| 1 cup | sun-dried cranberries | 250 mL |
| 1 cup | fresh wild blueberries | 250 mL |
| 2 Tbsp | Southern Comfort liqueur | 25 mL |

- Season turkey slices with salt and pepper. Rub a small amount of dijon mustard on both sides. Coat with pecan crumbs.
- In a skillet, heat safflower oil over medium heat. Cook cutlets on both sides, about 5 minutes in total, taking care not to brown the nuts. Serve with the fruit compote.

***Summer Fruit Compote***

- Bring honey and lemon juice to boil in a skillet.
- Add apricots and return to a boil.
- Reduce heat and add cranberries and blueberries. Heat through for 2 minutes. Remove from heat and add Southern Comfort.

For an exciting taste variation, try this recipe using wild turkey breasts. They can be obtained from Ken Rogers of Mount Forest, Ontario. *(See Source Information at back of book.)*

North Ridge Turkey Farm, Essex, Ontario, is a small-scale producer of turkeys, including cutlets, sausages and smoked and ground turkey, Although the birds are not certified organic, owner Velimir Baklic says, "I only sell what I would eat myself." Baklic feeds the birds a mixture of corn, soybeans and wheat, and does not administer hormones or antibiotics. North Ridge Turkey Farm will deliver to points as far away as Toronto. *(See Source Information at back of book.)*

*Since Grano opened in 1986, it has grown from a tiny, hole-in-the-wall Italian take-out and bakery, to a bustling 250-seat establishment, known for its twelve-foot antipasti counter. Diners immediately feel as if they have stepped into the home of owners and Italophiles Robert and Lucia Martella, and in some ways, perhaps, they have. (The Martellas live above the restaurant.)*

*Lucia Martella has always been responsible for all the menu planning and recipes, which she develops through a combination of research, adaptation of dishes served in her own home, and experimentation. "Many of the recipes we use in the restaurant," she says, "my mother used to make for me when I was growing up." The menu's soups, pastas and main courses change three to four times per year, as each season bestows new inspiration.*

*The boneless chicken breasts for this recipe are obtained from O.C.I.A.-certified Roth Family Farms in Picton, Ontario. They are a little larger and juicier too (a definite advantage when grilling them).*

# Grilled Stuffed Chicken Breast

LUCIA MARTELLA
Grano
*Toronto, Ontario*

SERVES 4

| | | |
|---|---|---|
| 4 | whole, boneless chicken breasts | 4 |
| 2–3 Tbsp | olive oil | 25–50 mL |
| 2–3 Tbsp | chopped parsley | 25–50 mL |
| 4–5 | large cloves garlic, peeled and puréed | 4–5 |
| | salt and freshly ground black pepper | |

| | | |
|---|---|---|
| ½ lb | shredded, smoked mozzarella cheese | 250 g |
| ½ lb | swiss chard, thoroughly washed, steamed, and well drained | 250 g |
| 12 | slices of pancetta (similar to bacon) | 12 |
| 2 | red peppers, roasted in a 400°F/200°C oven for 30 minutes, or seeded, quartered and grilled | 2 |

• Peel the peppers, then tear into strips about 1 inch/2.5 cm wide. Dress with 1 tsp/5 mL of the garlic, 2 tsp/10 mL parsley, salt and freshly-ground pepper.
• Prepare chicken breasts by removing all fat pieces and skin, if desired. Lightly season by coating with olive oil, parsley, garlic purée, salt and freshly ground pepper.
• Lay breasts out flat, or, if very thick, butterfly to open them out more.
• Place a layer of pancetta in the centre of the breast, then some chard, then some red pepper. Finish with a small handful of shredded smoked mozzarella.
• Fold the other half of the breast over to form a pocket. Wrap the breasts in foil and grill on a preheated hot grill (or under a broiler). When breasts are white all the way through, (about 5–10 minutes depending on heat of grill), remove the foil and set directly on the grill, briefly, to score the outside.
•Serve immediately as a main course or let cool and slice diagonally about ¼ inch/1 cm thick as part of a cold antipasto plate.

*Born in England's southeast county of Kent, (an area known as the Garden of England), John Rogers has devoted the last eighteen years to developing his personal culinary philosophy. In 1981, after completing the rigorous European chef's apprenticeship program and working for various hotels and restaurants throughout the United Kingdom, he relocated to Canada, where he settled in Vancouver.*

*In 1989, Rogers joined Windows on the Bay, the fine dining establishment in the flagship hotel of Coast Hotels and Resorts, as chef de cuisine. His seasonal menus draw heavily on the abundance of quality local and organic ingredients. In fact, Rogers has a standing arrangement with local supplier Herb Barbolet of Glorious Garnishes to send him "whatever happens to be at its best that week."*

*Located on the thirty-fifth floor of the hotel, the restaurant's spectacular panoramic view of English Bay, Stanley Park and the sparkling lights of Vancouver form a magnificent backdrop to John Rogers' innovative cuisine.*

# Roast Breast of Free Range Chicken with an Organic Redcurrant Ketchup

JOHN ROGERS
Windows on the Bay, Coast Plaza Hotel
*Vancouver, British Columbia*

SERVES 4

| | | |
|---|---|---|
| ¼ cup | virgin olive oil | 50 mL |
| 1 Tbsp | raspberry vinegar | 15 mL |
| 4 | large free range chicken breasts | 4 |
| | selection of organic salad leaves | |

*Ketchup*

| | | |
|---|---|---|
| ¼ cup | finely chopped red onion | 50 mL |
| 1 | large lemon — zest removed and juiced | 1 |
| 1 Tbsp | unsalted butter | 25 mL |
| 2 Tbsp | raspberry vinegar | 25 mL |
| 3 oz | fresh organic redcurrants | 90 g |
| 6 Tbsp | spring water | 90 mL |
| ¼ cup | brown sugar | 50 g |
| 1 tsp | grated fresh ginger | 5 mL |
| ½ | cinammon stick | ½ |
| | cayenne pepper and sea salt | |
| | fresh redcurrants for garnish | |

*Ketchup*

- Sauté onions and lemon zest in butter. Add vinegar, redcurrants and water. Bring to a boil and cook for 5 minutes.
- Add all other ingredients and simmer until the ketchup is reduced to approximately ¾ cup/175 mL, about 30 minutes. Season to taste.
- Blend the ketchup in a food processor until smooth. Allow to cool, overnight, if possible.

*Chicken*

- Preheat the oven to 325°F/160°C.
- Blend the olive oil with the raspberry vinegar. Just before cooking, dip the chicken in this oil and vinegar mixture.
- Roast the chicken breasts for approximately 20–30 minutes.
- Arrange a selection of seasonal salad leaves on four plates. Place the roasted chicken breast on the salad, sprinkle with the oil and vinegar dressing. Serve the redcurrant ketchup on the side, garnished with fresh redcurrants.

The restaurant obtains its chicken from Hills Foods Ltd. and redcurrants from Glorious Garnishes, both in the Fraser Valley. *(See Source Information at back of book.)*

*Despite numerous phone calls, I was not able to locate a certified organic supplier of duck. Leo Petipas of Mitchell, Ontario, with a flock of perhaps 200 Muscovy ducks, is currently aiming for certification and hopes to enter the market in 1993.* (See Source Information at back of book.)

*In general, farm-raised ducks (which can be any one of a number of varieties of the bird) are allowed to roam free in an open area, while those raised commercially are the more common Pekin variety, and are typically confined to cages. To qualify for certification, ducks would have to be fed certified feed, which is not widely available unless the farmer grows it himself on certified fields. Muscovy ducks are a favourite of chefs because they have comparatively low levels of body fat, and unlike chicken or turkey, contain all dark meat.*

# Crispy Duck Confit with Salad Greens and Blackcurrant-Hazelnut Oil Vinaigrette

BRYAN STEELE
The Old Prune
*Stratford, Ontario*

SERVES 4

***Confit***

| | | |
|---|---|---|
| 2 Tbsp | coarse sea salt | 25 mL |
| 1 | bay leaf | 1 |
| 12 | black peppercorns | 12 |
| 3 | allspice berries | 3 |
| 6 | juniper berries | 6 |
| 1 | small bunch fresh rosemary | 1 |
| 1 | small bunch fresh thyme | 1 |
| 1 | head garlic, halved, unpeeled | 1 |

| | | |
|---|---|---|
| 4 | large duck legs, preferably from Muscovy or Mallard ducks | 4 |
| 6 lbs | duck or goose fat* | 3 kg |

***Vinaigrette and Salad***

| | | |
|---|---|---|
| 2 Tbsp | blackcurrant vinegar | 25 mL |
| 2 Tbsp | heavy cream | 25 mL |
| 1 tsp | fresh blackcurrant purée (optional) | 5 mL |
| 2 Tbsp | hazelnut oil | 25 mL |
| | salt and freshly ground pepper | |
| 4 | handfuls mixed baby salad greens, such as Cookstown Greens | 4 |

• Several days before you intend to serve the duck legs, combine the salt, spices and garlic in a large bowl. Coat the duck legs with the mixture, then refrigerate them for two days, turning occasionally each day.

• Place the duck or goose fat, the duck legs, the marinade spices and the garlic in a large heavy pot. Over low heat melt the fat and continue heating until you can just see little bubbles breaking the surface. Adjust heat so that the duck legs continue to poach at a bare simmer and continue to cook for 2½ to 3½ hours, depending on the size of the legs. The legs are done when a skewer can pierce them very easily. When done, allow the duck legs to cool very slowly in the duck fat. This slow cooling is very important. (The confit can be prepared up to this point not only days but weeks or even months ahead, as long as care is taken to store the confit completely covered in fat in the refrigerator.)

***Vinaigrette***

• Whisk together the vinegar, cream and blackcurrant purée if desired. Slowly add the hazelnut oil in a fine stream whisking constantly. Do not use an electric appliance (such as a blender or food processor) for this, as the mixture might separate. Add the seasonings to taste.

• Remove the duck legs from the fat and set in a heavy skillet into which you have placed a bit of duck fat. Cook in hot (425–450°F/220–230°C) oven for 15 minutes, or until the skin is golden brown and crispy. Remove from oven and drain to remove excess fat.

• Meanwhile, mix the salad greens with some of the vinaigrette and arrange on plates together with the duck legs. Drizzle with the remaining vinaigrette and serve while the duck legs are still warm.

* Bryan Steele obtains goose fat by the pail from the Community of the Brethren, a religious community near Bright, Ontario. The Old Prune purchases ducks from Black River Game Farm, Pefferlaw, Ontario. *(See Source Information at back of book.)*

*"People would be surprised to know why I insist upon using organic chicken for this dish," says Steven James of Cafe Bruges in London, Ontario "With the organic chicken, you start out with an 8 oz/250 g breast, and cook down to 7 oz/200 g. With other chicken, I start out with an 8 oz/250 g breast and it cooks down to 4 oz/125g — it looks like something that came off a quail!"*

*James, who never went to culinary school, but has learned at the hands of such culinary stars as Anton Mosimann in London, England, is enthusiastic about the range of products obtainable from western Ontario producers. Five years ago, he says, you couldn't find the kinds of fish or mushrooms, for example, that you can get today. This choice has added a lot of regionalism to the things one can create in the restaurant. James likes to buy as many organically grown products as he possibly can, finding that "organic tastes better, is better for the environment and I like to support the local economy."*

*James opened Cafe Bruges in 1989 in his hometown, feeling that there was room for "something different to be done." The restaurant's name is inspired by his travels through Morocco and Belgium, where he met his Belgian-born wife, Maryanne.*

# Pan Seared Chicken Breasts with a Sweet Corn, Mushroom and Leek Succotash

STEVEN JAMES
Cafe Bruges
*London, Ontario*

SERVES 4

| | | |
|---|---|---|
| 2 | whole chickens, breasts filleted, legs removed and reserved (use the bones to make the stock, if desired) | 2 |
| | *or* | |
| 4 | boneless chicken breasts | 4 |
| 2 cups | chicken stock | 500 mL |
| 1 | clove garlic, chopped | 1 |
| 1 | carrot, diced | 1 |
| 1 | onion, diced | 1 |
| 1 cup | dried navy or white beans | 250 mL |
| 4 | ears of corn | 4 |
| 1 | leek | 1 |
| 1 | jalapeño pepper | 1 |
| 1 | poblano pepper (a mildly spicy Mexican pepper — if not available substitute 1 chili pepper) | 1 |
| 1 lb | oyster mushrooms | 454 g |
| 1 lb | mixture of green and yellow beans | 454 g |
| 2 Tbsp | fresh chervil, chopped, for garnish | 25 mL |
| 1 cup | unsalted butter | 250 g |
| 3 Tbsp | white wine vinegar | 50 mL |

• Soak the dried beans in cold water to cover, overnight, before proceeding with the recipe.
• Make a *mirepoix* by sautéing the garlic, carrot and onion in 1 Tbsp/15 mL of butter until soft.
• Roast the corn, husks on, in a preheated 400°F/200°C oven for 20 minutes. Remove the husk, scrape off the kernels and reserve in a bowl.
• Drain the beans, adding them with the vegetable *mirepoix* to the corn and mix. Dice the peppers and add to the bean-corn mixture. Pour the vinegar over the mixture and let it marinate.
• Slice the oyster mushrooms and reserve. French cut the beans and julienne the leek. Blanch the beans and leek in boiling water and rinse in cold water to retain bright colour.
• Heat 4 Tbsp/60 mL of butter in a sauté pan. When butter starts to foam, add chicken breasts one at a time, skin side down. Sauté until golden brown, then turn over to cook the other side. Cook until golden, but not so as to form a crisp skin on the bottom of the chicken. Place the chicken on a platter and keep warm.
• Pour off any excess fat from the pan and return to heat. Add 2 Tbsp/25 mL of butter, and then add the corn, bean and pepper mixture. Sauté lightly and then add the chicken stock. Over high heat bring the stock to a boil, and simmer, reducing by about half, adding the mushrooms, green and yellow beans, and leeks for the last few minutes of cooking. Do not cook off all the stock as you must whisk in some of the remaining butter to finish the sauce.
• Using a slotted spoon, place the succotash mixture on 4 warm plates and top with a warm chicken breast. Finish the sauce by swirling in pieces of the remaining butter and season with salt and pepper. Pour the creamy butter sauce over the chicken. Garnish with the chervil.

Steven James obtains vegetables from Encounter Farm Enterprises, Southwold, Ontario, and chickens from Robert Passmore, St. Marys, Ontario. *(See Source Information at back of book.)*

# MEAT

*Rabbit is an excellent choice for the health conscious as it is high in protein and low in fat and cholesterol. The Old Mahle House uses Vancouver Island rabbit for this dish. They reserve the loins for grilling, and braise the front and back legs.*

# Braised Rabbit with Oyster Mushrooms and Fresh Herbs

MAUREEN LOUCKS
The Old Mahle House
*Cedar, British Columbia*

SERVES 4

| | | |
|---|---|---|
| 2 | rabbits, cut up | 2 |
| | salt and pepper | |
| 2 cups | oyster mushrooms, sliced | 500 mL |
| 1 | clove garlic, finely diced | 1 |
| 1 | large onion, sliced | 1 |
| 1 Tbsp | dijon mustard | 15 mL |
| 4 cups | chicken or rabbit stock | 1 L |
| ¼ cup | fresh herbs: rosemary, sage, thyme, etc. | 50 mL |
| 1 Tbsp | olive oil | 15 mL |

• Season rabbit pieces with salt and pepper. Brown in olive oil over medium-low heat. When golden brown on both sides remove from frying pan and place in a roasting pan.

• If necessary add more oil to frying pan and lightly brown sliced onion and oyster mushrooms. Add garlic and dijon mustard, cook briefly, then add stock and chopped fresh herbs. Bring to a boil, then pour over the rabbit. Cover roasting pan and place in a 350°F/180°C oven for 45 minutes.

• Remove rabbit from pan and reduce liquid on high heat until desired consistency is reached.

*One of Stratford's most prominent sights, The Church Restaurant has been operating since 1975 when Joe Mandel purchased the building from a local congregation that was relocating. Chef/owner Sheldon Russell came to Canada to open the restaurant with Joe Mandel and has been associated with it ever since. Also the owner of Stratford's Keystone Alley Café, Russell bought The Church from Mandel in 1988.*

*Russell is passionate about organics and endeavours to use as many fresh and organically grown products "as I can get my hands on."*

# Barbecued Organic Lamb with Orange and Port Sauce

SHELDON RUSSELL
The Church Restaurant
*Stratford, Ontario*

SERVES 6

| | | |
|---|---|---|
| 2½ lbs | boneless lamb loin rolled and tied | 1.2 kg |
| | *or* | |
| 2¼ lbs | frenched lamb racks (whole) | 1 kg |

***Glaze***

| | | |
|---|---|---|
| 6 Tbsp | clover leaf honey | 100 mL |
| 2 tsp | balsamic vinegar | 10 mL |
| 2 | cloves garlic, roasted in their skins until soft, cut into two and squeezed | 2 |
| 1 Tbsp | chopped fresh rosemary | 15 mL |
| | zest of 1 orange | |

*Sauce*

| | | |
|---|---|---|
| 2 Tbsp | chopped shallots | 25 mL |
| 1 | clove garlic, chopped fine | 1 |
| 1 Tbsp | organic sunflower oil *or* | 15 mL |
| 1 Tbsp | butter | 15 mL |
| ½ cup | orange juice | 125 mL |
| | zest of 2 oranges | |
| ¼ cup | 35% cream | 50 mL |
| 1 cup | strained natural yogurt | 250 mL |
| 2 Tbsp | port | 25 mL |
| 1 Tbsp | chopped chives | 15 mL |
| 1 Tbsp | chopped rosemary | 15 mL |
| | sea salt | |
| | freshly ground pepper | |

- Place all ingredients for glaze in a bowl and mix together.
- Brush lamb with enough glaze to coat. Place in a preheated 350°F/180°C oven or on a medium-high barbecue.
- Roast to 130°F/54°C on a meat thermometer, basting with rest of the glaze as it cooks. (Approximately 45 minutes for loin and 30 minutes for the rack). Allow meat to rest for 20 minutes, keeping warm and saving natural juices.

*Sauce*

- Sweat shallots and garlic in the sunflower oil or butter until opaque. Add the orange juice and zest and reduce to ¼ of the original volume.
- Add the cream, ¾ of the yogurt, and bring to a boil. Simmer 1 minute. Allow to cool 1 minute, then whisk in the rest of the yogurt, port, herbs, and juice from the lamb (remove the fat). Season to taste and heat gently. Do not boil.
- Slice lamb as desired, accompany with sauce and serve.

The Church Restaurant obtains certified organic lamb from Larry Bender, Tavistock, Ontario. *(See Source Information at back of book.)*

# Escalopes of Venison, Raspberries and Lemon Balm with Roasted Shallots and Fiddleheads

ALAN GROOM
Bacchus Restaurant, The Wedgewood Hotel
*Vancouver, British Columbia*

SERVES 4

| | | |
|---|---|---|
| 8 | large shallots, skin on | 8 |
| 2¼ lbs | fiddleheads | 1 kg |
| 12 | escalopes of venison, taken from leg or loin | 12 |
| 2 Tbsp | olive oil | 25 mL |
| 1 lb | raspberries | 454 g |
| 1 tsp | sugar | 5 mL |
| 2 Tbsp | raspberry vinegar | 25 mL |
| 2 Tbsp | chopped lemon balm and a few sprigs for garnish | 5 g |

***Stock***

| | | |
|---|---|---|
| 3 lbs | venison bones, roasted | 1.5 kg |
| 3 | carrots | 3 |
| 1 | leek | 1 |
| 1 | stalk celery | 1 |
| | *bouquet garni:* fresh parsley, bay leaf and thyme, tied together | |
| | salt and pepper | |

***Stock***

• In a large pot, cover bones and vegetables with water. Simmer for 2–3 hours. Strain and reduce to two cups of glaze.

- In a 400°F/200°C oven, roast shallots for approximately 30 minutes, leaving whole. Leave skin on.
- Steam fiddleheads for approximately 10 minutes.
- In a heavy-bottomed skillet, quickly sauté venison in olive oil. Remove from pan (venison must be served rare).
- Place half the raspberries in the skillet. Sprinkle with 1 tsp/5 mL of sugar, and cook until slightly caramelized. Add raspberry vinegar and 2 cups/500 mL of the venison glaze. Reduce and strain. Reheat sauce gently, adding rest of raspberries. Add chopped lemon balm and remove from heat.
- Put fiddleheads on plate with shallots, split in half with skin left on. Set 3 venison scallops on top of fiddleheads. Top with sauce, garnish with a sprig of lemon balm, and serve.

The restaurant obtains venison from Arbutus Deer Farms, Mayne Island, British Columbia. *(See Source Information at back of book.)*

*English-born Kevin Snook delights in combing southwestern Ontario for sources of unique ingredients, a good deal of which is organically grown. "I hate salesmen — I much prefer to deal with the local guys," declares the affable Fox, who built his rustic, British pub-style restaurant himself just ten years ago. The restaurant's menu offers international selections in a casual atmosphere, and many of the daily specials feature local organic chicken, lamb, perhaps even wild boar, as well as vegetables. All of the herbs used in the kitchen come from the restaurant's own garden.*

# Grilled Lamb Sausages

KEVIN SNOOK
The Thirsty Fox
*Grand Bend, Ontario*

SERVES 6–8

| | | |
|---|---|---|
| 2¼ lbs | coarsely ground lamb shoulder | 1 kg |
| 3 | large eggs | 3 |
| ¼ cup | bread crumbs | 50 mL |
| 2 | cloves garlic, finely chopped | 2 |
| 1 Tbsp | each fresh parsley, chives, thyme, oregano | 15 mL |
| | freshly ground black pepper and salt | |

- Combine all ingredients and mix well. Divide into 6 equal portions.
- Form into desired shape and thickness. Place on a sheet of waxed paper and refrigerate until ready to use.
- Grill over hot coals to desired doneness.

Serve with Tomato–Rosemary Polenta (page 174).

*Although it is not widely known, calves that are raised to produce top-quality veal generally endure inhumane conditions from birth until they are slaughtered some twenty weeks later. Taken from their mothers at birth, the animals are confined in tiny stalls, where they have no room to move around (exercising causes their muscles to toughen, and the best-quality veal is extremely tender). In order to achieve the desirable white-coloured flesh, the calves are deprived of any iron, which is naturally present in their mother's milk and are instead fed a formula consisting of measured amounts of protein, vitamins and minerals.*

*In response to an outcry by the general public and animal rights groups, a producer in Charlevoix County, Québec is developing a method of raising calves that takes into account the total well-being of the animal, while also respecting the needs of the consumer.*

*The Charlevoix County calves are fed varying amounts of milk, grains and hay. The calves live in comfortable, quiet stalls, where they receive sixteen hours of light per day, and have plenty of room to run around. The result is a highly flavourful, top-quality product at a very competitive price.*

*"They have music to listen to as well," quips chef Dominique Truchon of Charlevoix County's Auberge des Peupliers, who uses Charlevoix County Veal exclusively. Truchon, who has been associated with the Auberge since 1983, and has served as its executive chef since 1985, is well known for his "cuisine regionale" — a menu that highlights producers from Quebec and the very bountiful Charlevoix County in particular. Freshness is a preoccupation of his, because, he says, "it produces almost flawless results." The Auberge, which has been in the Tremblay family since 1935, has been operating as a restaurant and inn since 1974, and carries on the family hospitality in impeccable style.*

# Escalopes of Charlevoix County Veal in a Lemon Thyme and Gruyère Crust

DOMINIQUE TRUCHON
Auberge des Peupliers
*Cap-à l'Aigle, Québec*

SERVES 4

| | | |
|---|---|---|
| 4 | medallions of veal, 5 oz/150 g each | 4 |
| | vegetable oil | |

***Crust***

| | | |
|---|---|---|
| ¼ cup | fine white bread crumbs | 56 g |
| 1 tsp | fresh lemon thyme, chopped | 5 mL |
| 3 Tbsp | butter, softened | 50 mL |
| 2 Tbsp | St. Fidèle gruyère, grated | 25 g |
| ½ | clove garlic, crushed | ½ |

***Sauce***

| | | |
|---|---|---|
| 1 | chopped shallot | 1 |
| 1 tsp | butter | 5 mL |
| 1 tsp | flour | 5 mL |
| ¼ cup | port | 50 mL |
| 1 cup | veal stock | 250 mL |
| | salt and pepper | |
| 2 tsp | butter | 10 mL |

***Crust***

• In a bowl, mix the bread crumbs, chopped lemon thyme, and a pinch of salt and pepper. With a fork or wooden spoon, combine with the softened butter, garlic and grated gruyère. Mix well, correcting seasoning if necessary.

*Sauce*

• In a skillet, sweat the shallot in 1 tsp/5 mL of the butter. Add the flour and cook over low-medium heat until golden in colour. **Do not brown.** Add the port and bring to a boil, allowing the alcohol to burn off. Whisk in the veal stock, simmer until slightly thickened, and stir in the remaining butter. Keep warm.

*Veal*

• Pan sauté on one side in oil, then place in an ovenproof dish with uncooked side up. Coat with the lemon thyme coating. Finish cooking in the pan and place under a broiler to brown if desired. Serve with the port sauce.

The restaurant serves this dish with parisienne potatoes, fan-cut carrots, and fiddleheads.

Charlevoix County Veal is located in St.-Agnes, Québec *(See Source Information at back of book.)*

*Serge Bruyère created this recipe for "A Celebration of Canadian Cuisine," the second annual benefit for the Stratford Chefs School, which was held in Toronto on March 1, 1992. The wild blueberries provide a delicate, tart flavour.*

*If caribou is unavailable, you can also make this recipe with beef fillet. Try to get unsprayed wild blueberries when they are in season. Several native bands harvest them and sell them through distributors in the south. You can freeze whatever you don't use.*

# Medallions of Caribou with Wild Blueberries

SERGE BRUYÈRE
À la Table de Serge Bruyère
*Québec City, Québec*

SERVES 4

| | | |
|---|---|---|
| 1½ lbs | caribou fillets, cut into 2½ oz/75 g pieces | 750 g |
| 3 Tbsp | sugar | 50 mL |
| 1 | shallot, chopped | 1 |
| ¼ cup | wine vinegar | 50 mL |
| 1¼ cups | veal stock (recipe follows) | 300 mL |
| ⅔ cup | wild blueberries | 150 mL |
| 15 | black peppercorns | 15 |

- To caramelize the sugar, put it in a heavy-bottomed pot and cook it over medium heat until it melts to a brown colour.
- Add the chopped shallots and half of the blueberries. Pour in the wine vinegar and veal stock. Simmer for 10 minutes.
- Pass the sauce through a fine strainer, mashing the blueberries against the side.
- Add the remaining blueberries to the sauce and keep warm.
- Pan fry the slices of meat in a hot pan for about 2 minutes per side. Serve the meat rare, topped with the sauce. Coarsely break or grind peppercorns over the meat and serve at once.

### *Brown Veal Stock*

| | | |
|---|---|---|
| 4–5 lbs | veal bones, cracked by the butcher or cut into pieces | 1.8–2.3 kg |
| 2 | onions, quartered | 2 |
| 2 | carrots, quartered | 2 |
| 2 | stalks celery, cut into 2-inch/5-cm pieces | 2 |
| 1 | chopped tomato (or 1 Tbsp/15 mL tomato paste) | 1 |
| | large *bouquet garni* (made with sprig of thyme, parsley and bay leaf laid on a piece of green leek, rolled and tied with a string) | |
| 1 | clove garlic | 1 |
| 10 | black peppercorns | 10 |
| 3–4 qts | water | 3–4 L |
| | non-aluminum stockpot | |

- Put the veal bones in a roasting pan and roast in the oven at 450°F/230°C for 30–40 minutes until well browned, stirring occasionally. Add the vegetables and brown them as well, 15–20 minutes longer. Thorough browning gives stock flavour and colour. For additional colour, singe half an onion over an electric plate or gas burner.
- Transfer the bones, vegetables and singed onion to the stockpot. Discard the fat from the pan and deglaze with 2 cups/500 mL water. Add the liquid to the pot, then make the stock. Add the chopped tomato or tomato paste, the garlic, *bouquet garni* and peppercorns.
- Bring slowly to a boil, skimming often. Simmer for 4–5 hours, skimming occasionally. *Note:* Stock should be reduced very slowly to avoid clouding.
- Strain and taste the stock. If the flavour is not strong enough, boil until it is more concentrated.

# Medallions of Roasted Venison Tenderloin with Sautéed Chanterelles

JOHN CRISTOU
Organics
*Toronto, Ontario*

SERVES 6

| | | |
|---|---|---|
| 2¼ lb | venison loin, cleaned | 1 kg |
| 1 Tbsp | peanut oil | 15 mL |
| 6 | whole shallots | 6 |
| | salt and pepper | |
| ¼ cup | organic red wine | 50 mL |
| 2 cups | spring water | 500 mL |
| 1 sprig | each of rosemary, thyme, parsley and tarragon | 1 sprig |
| 1 | bay leaf | 1 |
| 6 | whole black peppercorns | 6 |
| 2 | whole juniper berries | 2 |
| 2 oz | fresh chanterelles | 60 g |
| 1 Tbsp | butter | 15 mL |

- Preheat oven to very hot (450°F/230°C). Sear whole venison loin in hot peanut oil on all sides in a roasting pan.
- Add whole peeled shallots and sprinkle with salt and freshly ground pepper. Lower heat to 400°F/200°C. Roast venison and shallots in oven for 20 minutes or until rare. Remove from pan and let stand 5–10 minutes.
- Deglaze pan with red wine and add next 8 ingredients.
- Bring to a simmer and reduce by half. Strain through a fine sieve.
- Put whole shallots and any meat juices into blender, and purée.

- Sauté chanterelles in butter and season with salt and pepper.
- To serve, portion venison loin into 6 pieces, and top with the sautéed chanterelles and the sauce. Serve with Purple Potato and Garnet Yam Terrine (page 157).

# Wild Boar Loin with Mustard and B.C. Apples

PAUL ROGALSKI
La Chaumière
*Calgary, Alberta*

SERVES 4–6

| | | |
|---|---|---|
| 2¼ lb | wild boar loin | 1 kg |
| 1 | clove crushed garlic | 1 |
| 1 Tbsp | dijon mustard | 15 mL |
| 1 tsp | chopped fresh thyme | 5 mL |
| 1 tsp | chopped fresh rosemary | 5 mL |
| 1 tsp | chopped fresh marjoram | 5 mL |
| 1 tsp | crushed black pepper | 5 mL |
| | salt | |
| ¼ cup | all-purpose flour, preferably unbleached | 50 mL |
| 4 | small macintosh apples, cored and cut into rings | 4 |
| 1 cup | water | 250 mL |

- Preheat oven to 350°F/180°C.
- Clean wild boar of all fat and silver membrane.
- Rub the meat with crushed garlic and mustard, then sprinkle with the herbs and black pepper. Press them into the meat. Salt evenly.
- Roll the meat in flour, then place in a preheated, ovenproof frying pan and brown all sides evenly. Set pan in the oven for 15 minutes.
- Remove loin from the pan and keep warm.
- Add the apple rings to the same pan and bake until soft (approximately 5 minutes). Remove apples from the pan and add the water. Bring to a boil and strain.
- Slice the boar as thinly as possible and serve over the apple rings. Serve with the pan juices on the side or pour over the boar and the apples.

*"We are stewards of the land," says farmer John Rowe, whose Rowe Farm Meats sells chemical and hormone-free meats to individuals, restaurants and institutions throughout Ontario. "I'm just trying to do a better job and pass it on to the next generation."*

*The son of a veterinarian who sidelined as a federal meat inspector, John Rowe was raised with an awareness of the effects of hormones upon human health. In the 1960s, the Rowes became concerned when high incidences of cervical and vaginal cancer were beginning to appear in women who had taken the drug DES (diethylstilbesterol). At the time, DES was being widely administered to calves as a growth stimulant. (DES was subsequently taken off the market in the mid-1970s.)*

*Shortly thereafter, the Rowes began to raise a few cattle without hormones, antibiotics or steroids for their own use. By the mid-1970s, they were selling their naturally raised beef to the public. Today, they also raise pigs on their own land, where they cultivate clover, hay and small grains like barley, using organic methods. From an adjoining farm comes lamb, and other small farms in the vicinity supply chicken and turkey. Rowe maintains strict control over his few suppliers: he personally inspects each and every farm, and all are required to sign an affadavit guaranteeing the absence of any chemicals administered to the animals during their development.*

*"Conventional farmers are paid so little today that the only way for them to survive in beef farming is to be incredibly efficient. One way they can increase their efficiency is to give their animals whatever substances they can to induce them to mature earlier. Why are we doing this?" asks Rowe. "In the long run it saves the average family maybe $35 per person per year. Is it worth it in terms of the increased health risks we'll ultimately have to pay much more for? It seems pretty short-sighted."*

*"Change is pretty hard to effect, particularly at the educational level," he adds "The pharmaceutical companies will underwrite extensive research, knowing there's going to be a huge payback down the road. But who will underwrite organic farming? It just doesn't pay."*

*But Rowe is optimistic that public pressure can work to bring about the reduction in the use of these substances. "That's what I'd like to see over the next ten years or so," he says. "Producers moving toward the elimination of these things. I'm not trying to get people to eat meat if they don't want to. But for those who do want to I am offering a better quality product. We have a humanitarian obligation to give people the skills they need to survive. Globalization is a dangerous trend in food production. It only perpetuates a dependency on the big corporations, and eliminates our ability to be self-sufficient,"* he notes.

*A landmark in the small rural community of Dundas, Ontario, Picone's Food is a specialty grocery store that has been in the same family for four generations. Fresh, top-quality produce has always been the mainstay of the business, but in recent years the family has diversified, adding a variety of breads from local bakers from Oakville to Toronto, along with prepared foods such as salads, quiches and pies, which Mrs. Picone makes herself. Son Mark actively seeks out local organic growers and the store prominently features their products whenever they can.*

# Lamb Loin Chops with Seasoned Cracked Wheat

MARK PICONE
Picone's Food
*Dundas, Ontario*

SERVES 4

| | | |
|---|---|---|
| ½ cup | extra-virgin olive oil | 125 mL |
| 6 | cloves garlic, finely chopped | 6 |
| ½ cup | chopped fresh herbs, i.e., rosemary, thyme, oregano, marjoram, lavender, basil, fennel, savory | 125 mL |
| | zest from 2 lemons | |
| | freshly ground black pepper | |
| 2 | racks of lamb, cut into chops | 2 |

***Bulgur***

| | | |
|---|---|---|
| 2 Tbsp | butter | 25 mL |
| ½ | spanish (red) onion, finely chopped | ½ |
| 1 | bay leaf | 1 |
| 2 | cloves garlic, finely chopped | 2 |
| 1 | stick cinnamon | 1 |
| | salt and pepper | |
| 1 cup | bulgur | 250 mL |
| ½ cup | chopped dried apricots | 125 mL |
| ½ cup | dried tart cherries | 125 mL |
| 2 cups | water or stock | 500 mL |
| | fresh herbs for garnish | |

• Combine olive oil, garlic, herbs, lemon zest and pepper. Marinate lamb in mixture for 1 hour at room temperature.
• Preheat barbeque or grill.
• Melt butter and sauté onion, bay leaf, garlic and cinnamon stick in a skillet over medium heat for 3 minutes.
• Add bulgur, apricots and cherries and heat for 5 minutes or until lightly roasted. Add 2 cups/500 mL water or stock and simmer over low heat for 20 minutes.
• Grill the lamb on a hot barbecue or grill for 3–4 minutes per side. Keep warm.
• To serve, heap the wheat in the centre of plate or platter, surrounded by the lamb. Garnish with fresh herbs.

Mark Picone uses lamb from Rowe Farms. *(See Source Information at back of book.)*

*During the summer of 1992 Michael Stadtlander and his wife moved to British Columbia where they set out to fulfill a lifelong dream. "We want to buy a piece of land, raise our own chickens, ducks and pigs, have a little smokehouse, grow our own rice, and run an inn and a cooking school," he said to me, quite matter-of-factly, a few months before his departure.*

*Anyone who has known Stadtlander over the years knows that he has long been driven by his vision of natural things and is frequently given to such dreams. Having been raised on an organic farm in northern Germany, he has always possessed an affinity for the land. When he first came to Canada (to cook with Jamie Kennedy at Scaramouche in 1979) he was surprised to discover that Toronto was not the raw natural wilderness he had imagined this country to be. The various projects and enterprises he has been involved in since his arrival in Canada — Stadtlander's, Nekah, Knives and Forks, River Run, Feast of Fields, even his 1991 trip to several Japanese and Australian farms and wineries — all represent different stops on a journey back to the land.*

*"Wild foods are the best," he wrote to me from B.C., "You know, things like venison, pheasant, wild duck, squab, seaweed, wild mushrooms, and so on, and the next best things are of course organic, why, I don't have to explain to you."*

# Venison Chops with Wild Rice Noodles and Forest Mushrooms

MICHAEL STADTLANDER
April Point Lodge
*Campbell River, B.C.*

SERVES 4

***Sauce***

| | | |
|---|---|---|
| ¼ cup | olive oil | 50 mL |
| 2–3 lbs | bones and scraps from venison | 1–1.5 kg |
| 2 | parsnips | 2 |
| 2 | carrots | 2 |
| 1 | celeriac (celery root) | 1 |
| 2 | onions | 2 |
| 1 tsp | juniper berries | 5 mL |
| 1 | branch rosemary | 1 |
| 1 | branch thyme | 1 |
| 1 | bay leaf | 1 |
| 4 | cloves | 4 |
| 8 cups | chicken stock | 2 L |
| ½ cup + 2 Tbsp | cabernet sauvignon | 150 mL |
| 3 Tbsp | blackberry vinegar | 50 mL |

• Have the butcher chop the venison bones (or cut them yourself with a cleaver). Scrub all the vegetables and cut up into large pieces.

• Roast the bones in the olive oil in a roasting pan in a 400°F/200°C oven until golden brown, and then add the vegetables and garlic. Continue to roast, stirring occasionally, until everything is dark brown, and nicely caramelized. Remove pan from oven.

• Strain off the fat and deglaze with red wine. Add the chicken stock and bring to a boil. Skim off foam and add all the herbs. Let cook slowly on top of the stove for about 2 hours. Strain, and reduce to about 2 cups/500 mL. Set aside.

### *Wild Rice Pasta Dough*

| | | |
|---|---|---|
| 1½ cups | wild rice flour | 375 mL |
| 7 cups | hard white flour | 1.75 L |
| 3 | egg yolks | 3 |
| 4 | whole eggs | 4 |
| | salt | |
| 1 tsp | olive oil | 5 mL |

• In a large bowl mix the two flours. Stir in the rest of the ingredients and mix well. Knead until smooth. Let dough rest in the bowl for 1 hour. Roll the dough out in a pasta machine, cutting to ¼-inch/0.5-cm (fettucine-style) thickness. Set aside.

### *Venison Chops with Wild Mushrooms*

| | | |
|---|---|---|
| 7 Tbsp | butter | 90 mL |
| 4 | venison chops, 6–8 oz/ 175–250 g each | 4 |
| 6 | shallots, finely chopped | 6 |
| ¼ cup | blackberry vinegar | 50 mL |
| ½ lb | chanterelles or cèpes, or a mixture of both | 250 g |
| 1 Tbsp | chopped shallots | 15 mL |
| 1 tsp | chopped fresh thyme | 5 mL |
| 1 tsp | chopped fresh parsley | 5 mL |
| 1 Tbsp | chopped smoked bacon, optional | 15 mL |
| 12 oz | wild rice pasta (uncooked) | 375 g |

• Heat a large sauté pan, add 2 Tbsp/25 mL butter and sauté the venison chops slowly, turning once. When medium rare, set aside in a warm place (a 200°F/100°C oven is a good place).

• Fill up a large kettle with water and bring to a boil for the pasta. (Don't cook the pasta until you have completed the next step.)
• To the pan in which you sautéed the venison, add the 6 finely chopped shallots and caramelize them in 1 Tbsp/15 mL of butter. Then add blackberry vinegar and reduce. Add the 2 cups/500 mL of venison sauce and reduce until glossy.
• When the water boils, put in the pasta and cook until *al dente*. Drain and toss in 2 Tbsp/25 mL butter.
• Clean the mushrooms and slice. Sauté in 2 Tbsp/25 mL butter with the thyme, parsley and bacon, until tender.
• To serve, set 1 chop on each plate, accompanied by ¼ of the pasta and the mushroom sauté. Strain the sauce, and spoon on to the chops.

*Just an hour's drive from Toronto, in Cambridge, Ontario, lies William Bennett and Mary Beaton's exquisite country inn, Langdon Hall. It is here that European-trained chef Nigel Didcock (who honed his French technique at Pierre and Michel Troisgros' restaurant in Roanne, France) enjoys what must certainly be one of the most pleasurable experiences any chef could imagine. From the hotel's spectacular ¼-acre organic garden, lovingly tended by Matthew Smerek, comes much produce, including nineteen varieties of tomatoes, and eight kinds of kale. Chef and gardener work closely together to plan the garden. At the time of my visit, a new area was being cultivated to accommodate berries and currants. In another section of the property, a heritage orchard, containing old varieties of apples, had recently been planted.*

*In May 1992, Didcock invited me to accompany him on one of the hotel's traditional rites of spring, the annual hunt for morels in the two hundred acres of heavily wooded forest that encircle the inn and its magnificent gardens. The morels, explained Didcock, only appear for a brief two-week period in the middle of May, and the results of each expedition into the woods — which can be exhausting — are completely unpredictable. Slugs, deer and rabbits have all been known to feast upon the aromatic fungi. Since opening the inn's dining room in the spring of 1988, Didcock has kept a log of each year's harvest. The total harvest this year: a mere three pounds of morels.*

*"Spring is definitely the most exciting season here," said Didcock, as we stopped to snip a few fiddleheads on our way back to the kitchen. "It's a time of things beginning in the cycle of nature." Didcock incorporates each week's bounty into his menu, which changes every two months or so in keeping with his philosophy of serving "the season's best at the best time."*

# Sweetbread Terrine with Wild Leeks and Fresh Morels

NIGEL DIDCOCK
Langdon Hall
*Cambridge, Ontario*

SERVES 8

| | | |
|---|---|---|
| ½ lb | fresh veal sweetbreads | 250 g |
| 4 cups | veal stock | 1 L |
| 12 | wild leeks | 12 |
| ½ lb | morels | 250 g |
| 3–4 | shallots | 3–4 |
| 4 Tbsp | butter | 50 mL |
| 6 | gelatine leaves* | 6 |
| 2 | tomatoes, peeled, seeded and chopped | 2 |
| 1 cup | chopped fresh herbs: chives, italian parsley, chervil | 250 mL |
| 2 | egg whites | 2 |
| 1 | fennel bulb, sliced and marinated in ½ cup/125 mL of olive oil and 3 tbsp/50 mL lemon juice | 1 |

• Blanch sweetbreads by submerging in boiling water for 30 seconds, then set in a colander and refresh under cold water. Poach lightly in the stock for 5–8 minutes. Remove the sweetbreads and set aside.
• Clarify the stock as per the directions following. There should be 2 cups/500 mL of stock after clarification. Add a touch of port to the clarified stock if desired.
• Wash leeks, being careful to remove all sand, and trim ends, including 1 inch/2.5 cm of the tops. Blanch in boiling salted water and drain. Thoroughly clean morels, slice and sauté in

butter with the shallots. Season with salt and pepper. Cool.

• Soften the gelatine leaves for about 5 minutes in 1 cup/ 250 mL cold water. Drain, then combine with the 2 cups of clarified stock over gentle heat until completely dissolved.

• Build the terrine by placing several spoonfuls of dissolved gelatine in the bottom of a 2-quart/2-L creuset mold. Start with a layer of leeks, season with salt and pepper, add some of the herbs, and ⅓ of the sweetbreads. Sprinkle with some of the tomatoes, the morel-shallot mixture, and add a bit of the gelatine-stock mixture. Continue to layer in this matter to the top of the terrine. There should be 3 layers in all. Refrigerate for approximately 3 hours or until set.

• To serve, unmold, slice, then set on a bed of marinated fennel.

### *To clarify stock*

Beat the two egg whites in a mixing bowl, then add 1 cup/ 250 mL of the stock. Bring the remaining 3 cups of stock to a boil in a saucepan. While beating the egg white mixture, gradually add the hot stock in a thin stream. Pour the mixture back in to the saucepan and set over moderate heat, beating continually with a wire whisk. When it begins to simmer stop stirring. Continue to heat gently for 15 minutes. Strain through a cheesecloth.

*Professional chefs generally use gelatine leaves to set aspics and other molded dishes. If gelatine leaves are not available, substitute 2 envelopes unflavoured gelatine. Sprinkle the gelatine into ¾ cup/175 mL of cold water and let it soften for 3–4 minutes. Then combine with the stock over gentle heat until completely dissolved as in step 4.

# VEGETABLES AND SIDE DISHES

*A good accompaniment to the Medallions of Roasted Venison Tenderloin with Sautéed Chanterelles (page 142).*

# Purple Potato and Garnet Yam Terrine

JOHN CHRISTOU
Organics
*Toronto, Ontario*

SERVES 6

| | | |
|---|---|---|
| 2¼ lbs | purple potatoes | 1 kg |
| 2¼ lbs | garnet yams | 1 kg |
| 2 | eggs | 2 |
| | salt and pepper | |

- Scrub and peel potatoes and yams. Blanch in boiling water for 1 minute, then slice into ⅛-inch/3-mm rounds.
- Butter a small, ovenproof baking dish or terrine, and arrange alternating layers of the potatoes and yams.
- Beat eggs with salt and pepper. Pour into terrine. Cover with foil, leaving a small hole for venting.
- Set terrine into a larger baking dish that has been filled with boiling water, and bake in a 325°F/160°C oven for 45 minutes. Let stand 15 minutes before serving.

*Philippe Mollé is one of Montréal's most exciting and innovative chefs. Born in the French city of La Roche sur Yon, he began his career in Paris as an apprentice to chef Gaston Lenôtre before being hired by the Hôtel PLM St. Jacques. He then worked in Japan and Polynesia where he gained exposure to the tastes and flavours of the Pacific Rim. His restaurant in Tahiti, La Maison de Philippe, led him to develop friendships with such fascinating characters as Jacques Brel and Paul-Emille Victor.*

*In 1980, Mollé arrived in Canada to take charge of a vocational training program for teachers. In the following years, he represented the governments of Canada and Québec on several special missions to Louisiana, Japan, Abidjan and the Ivory Coast. In 1987, he opened the restaurant Le Saint-Honoré in Montréal which was awarded three stars in the 1988 Guide Debeur.*

*As the driving force behind the Hotel Vogue's stunning Société Café, Mollé's cuisine is continually evolving, reflecting the major factors that influence him: nutrition, quality, and a re-interpretation of the classics, with touches of Asian inspiration. An outspoken proponent of organic ingredients, he feels that they are healthier to eat, and uses them wherever possible.*

# Dried Bean Salsa with Fresh Herbs

PHILIPPE MOLLÉ
Société Café
*Montréal, Québec*

SERVES 6

| | | |
|---|---|---|
| ¾ cup | organic green lentils | 175 mL |
| ½ cup | organic green flageolets, (a rich-tasting green shelling bean, shaped like a kidney bean) | 125 mL |
| ½ cup | organic red kidney beans | 125 mL |

| | | |
|---|---|---|
| 2 | cloves garlic, finely chopped | 2 |
| 3 oz | organic tofu | 100 g |
| 3 Tbsp | hazelnut or walnut oil | 50 mL |
| 3 Tbsp | balsamic vinegar | 50 mL |
| 1 | tomato, finely diced | 1 |
| 6 | slices of rye bread | 6 |
| 18 | salad leaves | 18 |
| 2 Tbsp | chopped chives | 25 mL |
| | sea salt and pepper | |

• To prepare beans for cooking, wash each variety separately, picking them over carefully. Kidney beans and flageolets may be soaked overnight to shorten cooking time; lentils do not require pre-soaking. Simmer separately in lightly salted water or chicken stock until tender. Drain.

• Process tofu in a food processor with chopped garlic, hazelnut or walnut oil. With the machine running, drizzle in the vinegar, the beans and tomato. Season to taste.

• Toast rye bread and cut into croutons. Serve bean salsa on a bed of salad leaves topped with the croutons. Garnish with chopped chives.

*David Nobel obtains his fiddleheads from Ernie Hacquoil, a local bush worker who lives with his wife in Thunder Bay. Each spring, a field in the Hacquoil's backyard yields a bumper crop of fiddleheads — literally bushels of them. This inspired the Hacquoils to harvest them in quantity and sell them to local restaurants, markets and natural food stores. In the parking lot of the Neebing Road House, a local dining spot, Hacquoil and Nobel meet each spring to make the transaction, exchange recipes and talk shop.*

# Fiddleheads Parmesan

DAVID NOBEL
The Unicorn Inn
*South Gillies, Ontario*

SERVES 4–5

| | | |
|---|---|---|
| 1 lb | fiddleheads | 454 g |
| 2 Tbsp | kosher or coarse salt | 25 mL |
| 2½ Tbsp | fresh lemon juice | 40 mL |
| ½ tsp | concentrated liquid from soaking dried cèpes or boletus mushrooms (optional) | 2 mL |
| ¾ cup | freshly grated parmesan cheese | 175 mL |
| 4 Tbsp | unsalted butter | 50 mL |
| | salt and freshly ground black pepper | |

• Clean the fiddleheads (a hand-held dryer works well for this): Toss them in the air in batches, using the hair dryer (with the heat turned off or down) to blow away the majority of the brown husks. (Obviously, this is best done outdoors.) Then sort through and carefully remove any remaining husks.

• In a large pot, bring 4 quarts/4 L water to a boil. Add 2 Tbsp/25 mL kosher salt and 2 Tbsp/25 mL of the lemon juice, and return to a full rolling boil. Add the fiddleheads, cover, and parboil over high heat for 3 minutes. **Do not overcook, or fiddleheads will be bitter!**
• Drain the fiddleheads immediately and briefly refresh under cold water to stop cooking. Place in a colander and set aside to drain. This may be done up to several hours in advance.
• When ready to serve, preheat oven to 450°F/230°C, positioning rack toward the top of the oven. Butter the bottom of a casserole or baking pan with sides. Spread the fiddleheads evenly over the bottom. Mix the remaining ½ Tbsp/7 mL lemon juice and the cèpes liquid together and sprinkle over the fiddleheads. Season with salt and pepper. Sprinkle evenly with the parmesan. Dot with the butter.
• Place the pan in the oven and heat for about 10 minutes. Remove from the oven, cover loosely with foil, and return to the oven for 5 more minutes, or until the cheese is thoroughly melted and the fiddleheads are hot. Allow to settle a minute or two, adjust the seasonings, and serve.

You can find dried cèpes or boletus mushrooms in specialty food and Italian grocery stores. To make the concentrated liquid, soak a small package of dried mushrooms for half an hour in sufficient hot water to cover generously. Strain the liquid through cheesecloth into a small non-stick pan. (Reserve the mushrooms for another use.) Reduce carefully to a syrupy consistency. Any extra may be stored for up to two weeks in a tightly-covered container in the refrigerator. *(See Source Information at back of book.)*

*Despite the challenge of cooking both lunch and dinners six days a week in a 360-seat restaurant, Kurt Waldele is resolute in his determination to create innovative dishes using as many local and regional products as possible while promoting Canadian cuisine.*

*"Organic vegetables don't always look perfect," says the German-born Waldele, "but their taste is far superior to what is available commercially. We must support those people who are endeavouring to grow something different. If chefs don't support those people, they won't be around very long."*

# Mille-Feuille of Eggplant, Zucchini and Roasted Red Peppers

KURT WALDELE
Le Café, National Arts Centre
*Ottawa, Ontario*

SERVES 4

| | | |
|---|---|---|
| 1 | medium eggplant | 1 |
| 2 | medium zucchini | 2 |
| 2 | medium red peppers | 2 |
| 2 | medium cloves garlic, finely chopped | 2 |
| 1 | shallot, chopped | 1 |
| ¼ cup | olive oil | 50 mL |
| | salt and crushed black pepper | |

• Peel eggplant and slice thinly. Wash zucchini and slice lengthwise into thin pieces.
• Roast red peppers in hot (400°F/200°C) oven until charred and then peel off skins. Cut each pepper into 4 wedges and discard seeds. Season peppers with a little salt, pepper, garlic, shallots and olive oil. Set aside.

• In the meantime, season zucchini and eggplant with salt and pepper. Fry in a very hot cast iron skillet in olive oil until dark brown or almost black. Let cool.
• In a deep baking dish, alternately arange layers of eggplant, zucchini and red pepper on top of each other so as to form a loaf. Repeat layering procedure until all vegetables are used. Slice and garnish with a dollop of *crème fraîche* and deep-fried onion slices.

### *Crème Fraîche*

| | | |
|---|---|---|
| 1 cup | sour cream | 250 mL |
| 1 cup | 35% cream | 250 mL |

• Blend ingredients and allow to ferment at room temperature for 24 hours. Refrigerate.

### *Deep-Fried Onion Slices*

| | | |
|---|---|---|
| 1 | large yellow onion | 1 |
| | flour for coating | |
| 4 cups | olive oil | 1 L |

• Peel the onion and cut into fine slices. Sprinkle the slices with flour and deep fry in hot olive oil until golden brown and crisp.

*This dish makes a superb warm appetizer. Alternatively, it could be served as an accompaniment to a variety of grilled meats — such as a beef ribeye steak. (The restaurant uses organic beef exclusively — see note following recipe.)*

# Onion and Wild Mushroom Tart with Roasted Nuts

WOLFGANG VON WIESER
Four Seasons Hotel
*Vancouver, British Columbia*

SERVES 8

| | | |
|---|---|---|
| 6 | medium onions, sliced | 6 |
| 2 Tbsp | olive oil or clarified butter | 25 mL |
| 1 lb | wild mushrooms (i.e., chanterelle, oyster, shiitake), sliced | 454 g |
| ¾ lb | nuts, such as macadamia, brazil, or almonds (if using almonds, blanch first) | 375 g |
| ½ cup | 35% cream | 125 mL |
| ½ cup | sour cream | 125 mL |
| ½ lb | gruyère cheese, grated | 250 g |
| ½ bunch | chives, chopped | ½ bunch |
| | salt, pepper and nutmeg | |
| 1 | 10-inch pie shell, (unsweetened), pre-baked | 1 |

• Sauté onion in olive oil or clarified butter over low heat until very soft and golden brown. Drain off any excess liquid. Sauté sliced mushrooms until dry.

• Roast nuts in a slow (325°F/160°C) oven approximately 20 minutes or until golden brown and chop coarsely.

• Mix onions and mushrooms in a large mixing bowl together with the 35% cream, sour cream, grated cheese, chives, seasonings and chopped nuts.
• Pour mixture into pie shell and bake in a 350°F/180°C oven for approximately 15 minutes or until mixture appears slightly firm and is lightly browned on top.
• To serve, let tart cool completely in refrigerator, portion and rewarm in a 325°F/160°C oven for approximately 8-10 minutes.

The restaurant obtains mushrooms and onions from Hazelmere Farm in Surrey, B.C. Organic beef is supplied by Rodear Meats, Big Lake, B.C. *(See Source Information at back of book.)*

*British-born chef Keith Froggett is one of the reasons Scaramouche is one of Toronto's greatest dining experiences. Although Froggett modestly protests that he would prefer to "stay away from all the glitz and just serve people good food," his innovative compositions of regional ingredients are often dazzling, and the restaurant's impeccable service and magnificent views beckon us to return. A never-ending search for the most flavourful ingredients often leads Froggett to a number of small, local organic growers.*

# Ontario Morels filled with a Mushroom Mousse and Chive Beurre Blanc

KEITH FROGGETT
Scaramouche
*Toronto, Ontario*

SERVES 4

| | | |
|---|---|---|
| 8 | large fresh morels | 8 |
| ½ lb | mixture of paris, woodear, shiitake, and oyster mushrooms, diced | 250 g |
| 1 | clove garlic, chopped | 1 |
| 1 Tbsp | butter | 15 mL |
| 2 | chicken breasts, boneless and skinless, finely chopped | 2 |
| | salt, pepper and cayenne | |
| ½ | egg white | ½ |
| 1–2 Tbsp | 35% cream | 15–25 mL |
| 2 Tbsp | chopped herbs, such as parsley, thyme, chives | 25 mL |
| 1–1½ cups | chicken stock | 250–375 mL |

### *Beurre Blanc*

| | | |
|---|---|---|
| 4 Tbsp | shallots, peeled and finely diced | 50 mL |
| 2 Tbsp | white wine vinegar | 25 mL |
| ¼ cup | white wine | 50 mL |
| 7 Tbsp | butter | 100 mL |
| | juice of ¼ lemon | |
| 2 Tbsp | chopped chives | 25 mL |

• Pick over morels to make sure there are no insects inside. Try to avoid washing them if possible. Set aside.
• In a large pan, slowly cook the diced mushrooms with the garlic in the butter until they are very soft and have released all of their moisture. Squeeze them dry and save all the liquid. In a small pan, reduce the mushroom liquid to a glaze.
• Put the chicken meat in a food processor with the egg white, salt, pepper, a pinch of cayenne and the mushroom glaze. Run the machine until the whole mixture is smooth.
• Using the pulse action, slowly add a little cream to soften the mixture. Remove to a bowl set over ice and beat in enough cream to reach a consistency where the mixture just falls off a wooden spoon. Beat in the diced mushrooms and herbs and check seasoning.
• Using a piping bag, fill the morels. Lay them in a shallow pan and cover them halfway with chicken stock. Poach gently for about 5 minutes. Serve with the beurre blanc.

### *Beurre Blanc*

• Combine the shallots, vinegar and wine. Boil to reduce to about 1 Tbsp/15 mL and add a drop of cold water.
• Over low heat, whisk in the butter a little at a time to form an emulsion. Add a squeeze of lemon juice and the chives .

Although Scaramouche usually buys most of its wild mushrooms from Oishi Mushrooms, occasionally, says Frogget, during morel season, foragers will drive right up to the back door of the restaurant. *(See Source Information at the back of book.)*

*Tofino, a tiny community on the west coast of Vancouver Island, possesses "one of the most beautiful beaches in the world," according to Christina Delano-Stephens, owner of the town's Alley-Way Café, a casual place that caters to the many hikers and kayakers who frequent the area. Delano-Stephens, who is originally from Chile, was travelling in the area twelve years ago when she fell in love with it and decided to stay. The Tofino environment is so spectacular, says Delano-Stephens, that "we must take care of it and encourage other people to do so also." As the town is situated on a natural beach there isn't much soil to speak of. Consequently, all the restaurant's kitchen scraps go into a compost that Delano-Stephens has used to enrich her garden, where she grows many of the herbs that she uses in the restaurant.*

*"Organic food is definitely more flavourful and healthier to eat," says Delano-Stephens. "A few years ago, when I became aware of how animals were being raised, I took meat off the menu," she says. "But we are not a strictly vegetarian restaurant; we do serve some seafood," she adds.*

# Potato-Squash Enchiladas with Sour Cream Sauce

CHRISTINA DELANO-STEPHENS
The Alley-Way Café
*Tofino, British Columbia*

SERVES 6

| | | |
|---|---|---|
| 4 | medium organic potatoes, washed but not peeled | 4 |
| ½ | medium spaghetti squash | ½ |
| 1 | small onion, chopped | 1 |
| 2 Tbsp | cold pressed sunflower oil | 25 mL |
| | sea salt or salt | |
| 2 Tbsp | seaweed (kelp, hijiki or dulse) | 25 mL |
| ½ tsp | pepper (white or black) | 2 mL |

| | | |
|---|---|---|
| 1 tsp | chopped fresh basil | 5 mL |
| 12 | blue or yellow organic corn tortillas | 12 |

### *Sour Cream Sauce*

| | | |
|---|---|---|
| ½ | onion, finely chopped | ½ |
| | salt | |
| ½ tsp | chopped fresh basil | 2 mL |
| ½ bunch | finely chopped parsley leaves | ½ bunch |
| 1½ cups | sour cream | 375 mL |

### *Enchiladas*

• Cut potatoes in half and simmer until soft, approximately 20 minutes. Mash.

• Bake spaghetti squash in a 400°F/200°C oven for approximately 25 minutes, until the squash is soft. Scrape out the pulp. Mix with the potatoes.

• Sauté onion in safflower oil with salt, seaweed, pepper and basil. Mix with the potato-squash mixture.

• Lightly grill the tortillas. Put 2 Tbsp/25 mL of filling into the centre of each tortilla. Fold sides in to cover. Top with ¼ cup/50 mL of sour cream sauce and sprinkle with chopped fresh basil. Serve with a salad and a dry white wine.

### *Sour Cream Sauce*

• Sauté the onion with the salt, basil and parsley. When onion is translucent (about 2 minutes later), add the sour cream to the pan and heat through. Mix well and pour over the enchiladas.

*The best classically trained French chefs have always been closely connected to farmers, and naturally seek out the finest quality ingredients available. The same holds true for Dominique Crevoisier, who prefers to describe his cuisine as* naturelle *rather than "organic". After eight years of a varied apprenticeship that included time in France, England and Germany, Crevoisier came to Canada in 1975, where he has occupied various positions in restaurants and hotels from Edmonton to Québec. Established in 1971 by Parisians Ita and Jacques Landurie, the restaurant was named Les Halles to recreate the ambiance of the restaurants that were situated in that particular district of Paris.*

Artichauts violets dit poivrade *(small purple artichokes) are widely grown in the south of France, where they are typically prepared* à la Barigoule, *— in the manner described below. The leaves of this extremely tender artichoke are a dark shade of purple, and the whole choke can be eaten, unlike larger artichokes, whose only desirable flesh is found at the base of the leaves. At the end of July, the Montréal markets abound with these lustrous purple chokes, which come from local market-gardeners.*

# Small Purple Artichokes à la Barigoule

DOMINIQUE CREVOISIER
Les Halles
*Montréal, Québec*

SERVES 2

| | | |
|---|---|---|
| ¼ cup | olive oil | 50 mL |
| 1 | medium onion, sliced | 1 |
| 1 | carrot, cut into rounds | 1 |
| 8 | small purple artichokes, the stems trimmed | 8 |
| 1 | sprig thyme | 1 |
| ½ | bay leaf | ½ |

| | | |
|---|---|---|
| 4 | cloves garlic | 4 |
| ½ cup | dry white wine | 125 mL |
| 1 tsp | chopped parsley | 5 mL |
| 1 | sprig basil, chopped | 1 |
| | salt and pepper | |
| 1 | lemon, cut in half | 1 |

• Wash the artichokes and trim the stems and ends of the leaves. Rub the cut portions of the artichokes with the lemon.
• Heat the olive oil in a cast iron skillet. Cook the onions with the carrots until the onions are transparent.
• Place the artichokes on the bottom of the pan. Add the thyme, bay leaf, 2 whole cloves garlic and a bit of salt and pepper. Add the white wine and some water, just enough to cover the artichokes.
• Cook, covered, for 15 minutes over medium heat, just until the liquid has emulsified (the cooking liquid should be thick and syrupy). Remove from heat and season to taste.
• Chop the last 2 cloves of garlic and add, along with the parsley and basil. Mix carefully and serve.

*A streak of 60s-style idealism characterizes the history of Glorious Garnishes, suppliers of unusual produce to restaurants in the Vancouver area. The company's roots go back to 1977, when a group of thirty shareholders, united by "fantasy and philosophy" established a communal residence on a five-acre tract of land about one hour's drive east of Vancouver. Since then, the group has gone through a number of members and changing visions. But one of the original intentions — to try to create a livelihood for the group from the land itself — has held fast.*

*In 1984, a grant from the local Canada Employment Centre enabled the partners to begin developing, at the request of Isadora's Co-op Restaurant, a prototype salad, containing some thirty different ingredients. The salad, which contains edible wild greens, shepherd's purse, herbs, shiso, sorrel and edible flowers, was inspired by a similar one produced by Mark Musick of Pragtree Farm in Washington State at that time. Today, the original mixture has evolved into the company's Celebration Salad, which, along with the ten-ingredient Mesclun Mix, forms the mainstay of the company's revenue. Specialty herbs, and other eclectic produce such as salmon berries and wild dandelions, are offered as they are available.*

*The idealism that underlay the company from its inception runs true today, as the partners continue to grapple with some of the most pressing issues in modern agriculture. "People can't ignore the realities any more," says Susan Davidson, one of the company's founding partners and a member of the cooperative that operates the salad company. "People object to paying higher prices for organically grown food, but that is because they don't understand the ecological implications of growing cheap food."*

# Steamed Greens

HERB BARBOLET
The Glorious Garnish and
Seasonal Salad Company
*Aldergrove, British Columbia*

SERVES 4

| | | |
|---|---|---|
| 1 per person | large handful raw greens, including: amaranth, arugula/rocket, beet tops, chard, kale, mizuna, mustards, shingiku, spinach | 1 per person |

- In a kettle large enough to accomodate the greens, heat 1 inch/2.5 cm of water to boiling. Steam greens using either a wire basket or bamboo steamer for about 1 minute. Kale should retain its brilliant green colour.
- Serve plain, or with butter, lemon or dressing.

***Dressing***

| | | |
|---|---|---|
| ¼ cup | light soy sauce | 50 mL |
| 1½ cups | vegetable oil | 375 mL |
| 2–3 cloves | crushed garlic cloves | 2–3 cloves |

- Combine all ingredients and mix well.

Options: substitute part sesame oil, add sesame seeds, poppy seeds and/or grated ginger.

*Kevin and Marilyn Snook spend half the year in Grand Bend, a casual resort community on the southern shore of Lake Huron, where they are participating in a pilot project involving recycling in commercial establishments. From October to April they live in France, where they work, study, and continue to enrich their appreciation of food and wine.*

*Serve this tasty polenta with Kevin Snook's famous Grilled Lamb Sausages (page 136).*

# Tomato–Rosemary Polenta

KEVIN SNOOK
The Thirsty Fox
*Grand Bend, Ontario*

SERVES 8

| | | |
|---|---|---|
| 2 | large ripe tomatoes, peeled and seeded | 2 |
| 5 cups | chicken stock | 1.2 L |
| 4 | sprigs fresh rosemary | 4 |
| 1½ cups | yellow cornmeal | 375 mL |
| 2–3 Tbsp | butter | 25–50 mL |
| ¼ cup | parmesan cheese | 50 mL |
| ¼ cup | olive oil, for oiling pan | 50 mL |
| | salt and freshly ground black pepper | |

- Purée tomatoes in blender or food processor for 1 minute until smooth.
- Bring chicken stock and rosemary to a boil. Simmer for 5 minutes, then remove the rosemary.
- Over low heat gradually whisk in cornmeal and simmer for 15 minutes. Remove from heat and stir in all other ingredients except the oil. Season to taste.

• Turn onto a lightly oiled, 9-inch/23-cm square pan (or non-stick jelly roll pan) and cool.
• Just before serving brush with a little olive oil and grill or bake for an additional 10 minutes, if desired.

Organically grown, stone ground cornmeal from Oak Manor Farms is available at health food stores. *(See Source Information at back of book.)*

*Isadora's Co-op Restaurant was founded in 1982 by a group of people in the Granville Island area who wanted to establish a restaurant that served high-quality West Coast cuisine at affordable prices. Funded by the sale of 1,500 cooperative shares to people in the community, the unconventional concept was a terrific success right from the beginning. Since its first year of operation, the restaurant has been busy, according to chef Hubertis Surm.*

*The amount of organic products used has grown over the years as Surm, who has always been interested in raising things naturally, has developed a more extensive network of local suppliers. During the mid-1980s the restaurant worked closely with Glorious Garnishes to develop their Celebration Salad Mix.*

# Isadora's Autumn/Winter Vegetable Lasagna

HUBERTIS SURM
Isadora's Co-op Restaurant
*Vancouver, British Columbia*

SERVES 8

| | | |
|---|---|---|
| 4 | sheets fresh lasagna pasta | 4 |
| 2 lbs | butternut squash, peeled and sliced | 1kg |
| 2 | medium eggplants, one cut into ½-inch/1-cm thick slices, the other in ½-inch/1-cm cubes | 2 |
| 2 | medium zucchini, sliced lengthwise into ¼-inch/½-cm slices | 2 |
| 1 Tbsp | lemon juice | 15 mL |

***Sauce***

| | | |
|---|---|---|
| 2 cups | finely diced onion | 500 mL |
| 2 Tbsp | crushed garlic | 25 mL |

| | | |
|---|---|---|
| 1 Tbsp | cumin | 15 mL |
| ½ Tbsp | black pepper | 7 mL |
| 2 Tbsp | paprika | 25 mL |
| pinch | cinnamon | pinch |
| dash | tabasco | dash |
| 1 Tbsp | olive oil | 15 mL |
| 1 cup | tomato sauce | 250 mL |
| 1 | green pepper, finely diced | 1 |
| ½ | red pepper, finely diced | ½ |
| 1 Tbsp | lemon juice | 15 mL |
| | olive oil | |
| | salt | |
| ½ lb | ricotta cheese | 225 g |
| 1 cup | freshly grated parmesan | 250 mL |
| 1 cup | monterey jack cheese, grated | 250 mL |

- Cook lasagna noodles in boiling water for 3 to 5 minutes. Drain and cool.
- Slice butternut squash into ¼-inch/0.25-cm thick slices and steam for 5 minutes. Steam eggplant cubes for 5–7 minutes.
- Grill eggplant and zucchini slices and season with salt, fresh pepper and a little lemon juice.

### *Sauce*

- Sauté onions, garlic, cumin, paprika, cinnamon and tabasco for 5–7 minutes, in olive oil. Add tomato sauce, cubed eggplant, red and green peppers and lemon juice. Cook until mushy, remove from heat and cool.
- *To assemble*: Oil the bottom of an 8 x 12-inch/20 x 30-cm pan. Place a layer of noodles on the bottom of the pan, then continue layering with eggplant slices, half of the sauce, one third of the parmesan and ricotta. Top with a layer of noodles, then all the butternut squash, another one third of the parmesan and ricotta, another layer of noodles, all of the zucchini, the remaining sauce, one third of the parmesan and ricotta and top with all of the monterey jack cheese.
- Bake at 350°F/180°C for 20 minutes.

*Capers is a seven-thousand-square foot eco-store, featuring a large variety of organic meat, produce and groceries, as well as environmentally sound household products. The in-store restaurant, which began as a twenty-seat café serving coffee, muffins and light lunches in 1985, has grown into a three-meal-a-day, seventy-seat gourmet restaurant with a deck that overlooks Vancouver's beautiful English Bay. During lunch and dinner hours, a line of twenty to thirty people can wind through the store. The store also has a full-service deli counter, which uses organic ingredients wherever possible, and complete bakery, meat and seafood counters.*

*Chef Rick Maddison, who has been the restaurant's managing chef since 1989, is responsible for developing a menu that caters to a wide range of tastes, from strict vegetarian to fish and meat lovers. Every day, the deli features a dozen different salads, three soups, even roast beef sandwiches made from organically-raised beef, which is roasted in the store.*

*Store manager Russell Precious has been involved in organic farming and wholesaling for more than twenty years, and has built strong ties with the local farming community. Interestingly, Precious has discovered that "environmentalism is doing more to change people's eating habits than concern over health ever did."*

# Whole Wheat Udon Noodles with Napa Cabbage, Tofu and Toasted Nori

RICK MADDISON
Capers
*Vancouver, British Columbia*

SERVES 4–6

| | | |
|---|---|---|
| ⅓ cup | roasted sesame oil | 75 mL |
| ¼ cup | apple cider vinegar | 50 mL |
| ⅓ cup | tamari (soy sauce) | 75 mL |
| 3 Tbsp | honey | 50 mL |

| | | |
|---|---|---|
| 1 lb | udon noodles | 454 g |
| 14 oz | pressed tofu | 400 g |
| 1 | napa cabbage, coarsely chopped | 1 |
| 2 Tbsp | sesame oil | 25 mL |
| 2 Tbsp | roasted sesame seeds | 25 mL |
| 2 | sheets nori seaweed, toasted and crumbled (see note following) | 2 |

- In a small bowl, combine sesame oil, apple cider vinegar, tamari and honey.
- Cook noodles in lightly salted water until tender, about 8 minutes.
- Sauté tofu and cabbage in 2 Tbsp/25 mL sesame oil until cabbage is wilted.
- Toss cabbage, tofu and noodles together and add sauce. Divide on plates and top with sesame seeds and nori.

*Note*: Wave nori sheets over hot element or open flame until they begin to break. After cooling nori will become brittle and easy to crumble.

All the ingredients used in this recipe can be obtained at Capers. (*See Source Information at back of book.*)

*Paul Boehmer devised this winter vegetable cake during his term at The Parrot in Toronto, while experimenting with creating a fully organic menu. One of my favourite treatments for winter vegetables, it is simple to prepare yet very flavourful.*

*Paul is an enormously talented chef with a penchant for freshness and quality. He cites Michael Stadtlander as a major influence in his approach to cooking, having worked with him at both Stadtlander's and Nekah. At Opus Restaurant, which he opened during the summer of 1992, Paul's cooking continues to reflect the elements that earned his reputation: fresh, seasonal ingredients, cream-free sauces and distinctively French influences.*

# Winter Vegetable Cake

PAUL BOEHMER
Opus Restaurant
*Toronto, Ontario*

SERVES 10–12

| | | |
|---|---|---|
| 10 | shallots, finely chopped | 10 |
| 5 | medium potatoes, thinly sliced | 5 |
| 2 | large carrots, thinly sliced lengthwise | 2 |
| 2 | large beets, thinly sliced | 2 |
| 1 | medium celery root, scrubbed, peeled and thinly sliced | 1 |
| ½ cup | butter | 125 mL |
| | salt and white pepper | |

- Butter a deep glass pie plate. Sprinkle ⅕th of the shallots over the plate and up the sides; season with salt and pepper.
- Put all the potatoes in one layer, top with a sprinkle of shallots, salt, pepper, and thin slices of butter.

• Put all the carrots in the next layer, topping with shallots, seasoning and butter.
• Do the same with the next layer, using the beets.
• The final layer is the celery root, also sprinkled with shallots, salt, pepper and butter.
• Cover with aluminum foil and bake at 375°F/190°C for 40 minutes.
• The cake should be up to 1½ inches/3.5 cm thick. It can be cut into 10–12 portions and served as one of the accompaniments to a variety of main dishes. The cake reheats very well, and can be refrigerated for about a week.

## Winter Vegetable Casserole

KAREN BARNABY
Raintree Restaurant
*Vancouver, British Columbia*

SERVES 4–6

| | | |
|---|---|---|
| ¾ lb | potatoes, peeled and cut into 1-inch/2.5-cm cubes | 360 g |
| ¾ lb | rutabaga, peeled and cut into 1-inch/2.5-cm cubes | 360 g |
| ¼ lb | carrots, peeled and cut into ¼-inch/5-mm cubes | 120 g |
| 1 lb | savoy cabbage, cored and cut into ½-inch/1-cm slices | 454 g |
| 1 tsp | salt | 5 mL |
| | ground black pepper | |
| ½ lb | cream cheese | 225 g |
| 1 Tbsp | unsalted butter | 15 mL |

• Preheat the oven to 350°F/180°C. Place all the vegetables in a large pot and cover with cold water. Bring to a boil and cook until the potatoes are tender. Drain well and place vegetables back in the pot. Mash coarsely with a potato masher.

• Stir in the salt, pepper, cream cheese and butter. Transfer to a buttered casserole dish and smooth the top. Bake for 45 minutes until the top is lightly browned.

*The perfect accompaniment to Paul Rogalski's Wild Boar Loin (page 144).*

# Red Alsatian Cabbage

DOMINIQUE CREVOISIER
Les Halles
*Montréal, Québec*

SERVES 6

| | | |
|---|---|---|
| 1 | medium head red cabbage | 1 |
| pinch | sugar | pinch |
| 1 Tbsp | red wine vinegar | 15 mL |
| 6 Tbsp | duck fat | 90 mL |
| 1 | large onion, finely chopped | 1 |
| 1 cup | red wine | 250 mL |
| 1 | bay leaf | 1 |
| 4 | apples, peeled and cut in large dice | 4 |
| | salt and pepper | |

• Cut the red cabbage into julienne and let marinate overnight with the salt, sugar and wine vinegar.
• The next day, heat the duck fat in a large skillet and sweat the onions for 4–5 minutes until they are transparent. Add the red cabbage. Cook for 5 minutes and deglaze with the red wine. Stir well and taste for seasoning. Add the bay leaf.
• Cover and cook in the oven at 325°F/160°C for 1 hour. Add the apples and continue to cook for another hour and 15 minutes. All the liquid should be evaporated.

*Brian Clafton was one of the first chefs in Toronto to use organic ingredients in the kitchen of a major hotel. Despite the fact that throughout 1991 the hotel was undergoing extensive renovations, forcing him to rely on vacuum packs for the cooking and reheating of some dishes, Clafton's menu changed almost weekly and was comprised of over ninety percent organic ingredients — a rarity, particularly in a hotel kitchen.*

*Clafton no longer highlights items as "organic," having found that "people perceive organic food as being more expensive and don't want to pay for an advantage that they can't always detect." However, recognizing the superior quality and flavour of these products, Clafton continues to use chemical-free meat and eggs exclusively in his kitchen, and seasonal, frequently organic, vegetables continue to figure prominently in his menus.*

## Vegetarian Sandwich

BRIAN CLAFTON
Ramada Renaissance on Bloor
*Toronto, Ontario*

SERVES 4

| | | |
|---|---|---|
| 1 | each of zucchini, eggplant, onion, carrot, green or red pepper | 1 |
| ¼ cup | olive oil | 50 mL |
| 1 Tbsp | balsamic vinegar | 15 mL |
| 4 | pitas (flat bread) | 4 |
| 3 Tbsp | tahini (sesame seed paste) | 50 mL |
| ½ cup | hummus (recipe follows) | 125 mL |
| 1 cup | tabbouleh (recipe follows) | 250 mL |
| | handful sunflower seedlings | |

• Clean and slice vegetables lengthwise. Place vegetables on a baking sheet, toss with 1 Tbsp olive oil and roast in 400°F/200°C oven until cooked but crisp, about 20–30 minutes.
• Cool and slice into fork-sized pieces, and toss with a vinaigrette made from 3 Tbsp/50 mL olive oil and 1 Tbsp/15 mL balsamic vinegar.
• To assemble, spread split pita halves with some tahini, then hummus, then add tabbouleh and vegetables. (Sandwich can be warmed in a microwave if desired). Top with sunflower seedlings and roll like a tortilla, securing with a toothpick. Serve with a light salad, chips or whatever you fancy.

### *Hummus*

| | | |
|---|---|---|
| ½ cup | dried chick peas or ½ can cooked chick peas, drained | 125 mL |
| 7 Tbsp | freshly squeezed lemon juice, or more to taste | 100 mL |
| ½ tsp | chopped garlic | 2 mL |
| 7 Tbsp | tahini (sesame seed paste) | 100 mL |
| ½ tsp | salt | 2 mL |
| 1 Tbsp | olive oil | 15 mL |

• If using dried chick peas, soak overnight in water to cover. Drain; rinse well. Cook in simmering water, covered, about 1½ hours or until tender. Drain.

### *Couscous Tabbouleh*

| | | |
|---|---|---|
| ½ cup | couscous | 125 mL |
| 1½ cups | boiling water | 375 mL |
| 2 | cloves garlic, chopped | 2 |
| 1 Tbsp | olive oil | 15 mL |
| ½ cup | chopped parsley | 125 mL |
| 1 | whole tomato, seeded and diced | 1 |
| 3 | green onions, chopped | 3 |

- Soak couscous in boiling water for 5 minutes, covered. Drain, if necessary,
- Stir in garlic and olive oil
- Cool and add parsley, tomato, and chopped green onion.

- Process the lemon juice with the garlic in a food processor or blender. Add the chick peas, a handful at a time. Gradually add the tahini paste, olive oil, and a couple of spoonfuls of water. When the purée is smooth and creamy, adjust the seasoning with more salt, garlic or lemon juice to taste.

Organic pitas are available at The Big Carrot and Alternatives. Sunflower seedlings may be purchased from Cookstown Greens. *(See Source Information at back of book.)*

# DESSERTS

*What more delightful way to enjoy fresh strawberries in season — particularly when the chef grows them himself — than to imbibe them in this frothy concoction of berries, cream and champagne.* À votre santé!

# Minted Strawberry Syllabub

WERNER BASSEN
Acton's Grill and Café
*Wolfville, Nova Scotia*

SERVES 6

| | | |
|---|---|---|
| 1 quart | fresh strawberries, hulled and puréed | 1.2 L |
| 3 cups | whipped cream | 750 mL |
| ½ cup | sugar | 125 mL |
| ½ cup | dry sherry | 125 mL |
| ¼ cup | brandy | 50 mL |
| 1 cup | dry champagne | 250 mL |
| 2 Tbsp | finely chopped fresh mint | 25 mL |

• Whisk all ingredients together and refrigerate for at least 4 hours. Just before serving, whisk again and pour into champagne flutes.

Acton's uses strawberries from its own farm for this "spoon and drinking" dessert.

*I was wondering where in Edmonton I might find a chef or two so enlightened as to seek out local, organically grown ingredients, when a friend told me about The Unheard Of, a memorable restaurant she had eaten in several years ago. During the summer, proprietors David and Lynn Heard obtain most of the herbs, tomatoes, potatoes, carrots and peas that are used in the restaurant from their own nearby garden. Because the growing season is so short, the restaurant's emphasis is on winter foods, and the Heards make all their own relishes and chutneys, which they serve along with such specialties as game, duck and root vegetables. If you are lucky enough to enjoy their extraordinary six-course prix-fixe meal, be sure to leave room for one of their fabulous desserts.*

# Apple Phyllo Supreme

DAVID HEARD
The Unheard Of
*Edmonton, Alberta*

SERVES 10

***Phyllo pastry***

| | | |
|---|---|---|
| 4–5 | 12 x 18-inch/30 x 46-cm sheets packaged phyllo dough | 4–5 |
| ½ cup | melted butter | 125 mL |

***Filling***

| | | |
|---|---|---|
| 8 | fresh apples | 8 |
| 2 Tbsp | brandy | 25 mL |
| ½ cup | brown sugar | 125 mL |
| pinch | cinnamon | pinch |
| 2 tsp | butter | 10 mL |
| 1 Tbsp | cornstarch | 15 mL |

***Pastry cream***

| | | |
|---|---|---|
| ½ cup + 2 Tbsp | sugar | 150 mL |

| | | |
|---|---|---|
| 4 | egg yolks | 4 |
| ¼ cup | flour | 50 mL |
| 1½ cups | milk | 375 mL |
| 1 tsp | vanilla | 5 mL |
| | whipped cream and melted chocolate for garnish | |

• Line the sides of a 9-inch/23-cm flan pan with a removable bottom with parchment paper so that the paper comes over the fluted edge. (The bottom will sit over the paper liner.) Cut a round of paper to fit the bottom of the flan pan insert.
• Make a pie crust out of the phyllo: Cut the sheets of phyllo into 4 equal rectangular pieces. Then cut 2 of the 4 rectangles in half again. Take 2 of the 6 x 9 inch/15 x 23 cm pieces, brush them with melted butter, and set them, buttered side down in the prepared pan. Then line the edge with the strips of phyllo, which you have buttered. Continue alternating until pastry is used up.
• Cut excess from the rim area and prick bottom. Cover with parchment paper and weigh down. Bake at 350°F/180°C for 10 minutes or until phyllo is crisp and brown. Cool and set aside.
• While crust is baking, prepare apple filling: peel and core apples and cut into 1-inch/2.5-cm dice. Simmer with brandy, brown sugar, cinnamon, and butter. When mixture has reached a soft consistency, pour off some of the liquid into a small measuring cup, and add 1 Tbsp/15 mL cornstarch to the removed liquid. Add dissolved cornstarch mixture back to sauce and cook until thickened. Cool.
• *Pastry cream:* In a double boiler, combine sugar and eggs, beating until thick and foamy. Add flour, scalded milk and vanilla. Cook, stirring constantly, until thickened, then cool.
• *Assembly:* Spoon apple sauce into crisp pastry shell, and top with ¾–1 cup/175–250 mL pastry cream. Finish by outlining 10 portions with sweetened whipped cream using a pastry bag and a star tube. On serving plate, garnish each portion with squiggles of melted chocolate.

Serve chilled, within 2–3 hours, or crust will become soggy.

*Butter tarts are a Canadian tradition and this luscious variation will soon become a favourite of yours. Don't think about the calories, just savour every sinfully delicious bite!*

# Butter Tart Flan

DAVID HEARD
The Unheard Of
*Edmonton, Albert*

SRVES 10–12

| | | |
|---|---|---|
| 1 | 10–12 inch/25–30 cm pastry shell (use recipe following, or your favourite pie crust recipe) | 1 |

***Filling***

| | | |
|---|---|---|
| 3 | eggs | 3 |
| 2 cups | brown sugar | 500 mL |
| 1 cup | melted butter | 250 mL |
| 2 tsp | white vinegar | 10 mL |
| ½–1 cup | currants or yellow raisins | 125–250 mL |
| ½ cup | walnuts (optional) | 125 mL |

***Custard***

| | | |
|---|---|---|
| 4 | egg yolks | 4 |
| ⅓ cup | sugar | 75 mL |
| 1 Tbsp | flour | 15 mL |
| 2 cups | 35% cream | 500 mL |
| | 35% cream, whipped | |

***Pie Crust***

| | | |
|---|---|---|
| 2 cups | soft organic white flour | 500 mL |
| ½ tsp | salt | 2 mL |
| ¾ cup | unsalted butter, chilled, and cut into small pieces | 175 mL |

| | | |
|---|---|---|
| 3 Tbsp | vegetable shortening | 45 mL |
| 3–4 Tbsp | ice water | 45–60 mL |

*Pie Crust*

• Put the flour and salt into the bowl of a food processor. Pulse once or twice to mix. Add the pieces of butter to the bowl and process until mixture resembles coarse crumbs. With the machine running, add the water drop by drop, until dough just holds together.

• Turn the dough out onto a lightly floured smooth surface or onto a piece of waxed paper. Using the heel of your hand press down on the dough several times and then gather it all up into a ball. Wrap up tightly in waxed paper and chill for at least 1 hour or overnight.

• Roll with a floured rolling pin into a large circle, 1 inch/ 2.5 cm larger in diameter than your baking dish. Place pastry in pan and press into sides. Use rolling pin to trim off excess.

• Bake the pastry shell in a preheated 350°F/180°C oven for 12 minutes.

• While it is baking, make the butter tart filling. Whisk the eggs with the brown sugar, melted butter and white vinegar.

• Into the partially baked pie shell, sprinkle the currants and/or walnuts (if used). Then pour in the filling. Bake at 350°F/180°C for 20 minutes.

• While the flan is baking, make the custard: in a double boiler over simmering water, combine the egg yolks, sugar, flour and 2 cups/500 mL heavy cream. Stir continuously until thickened, then remove from the heat and set aside.

• Remove the flan from the oven, and lower the oven temperature to 300°F/150°C. Spread the custard over the flan and bake for an additional 30 minutes.

• To serve, garnish with the whipped cream.

*The Heritage Seed Program, a project of the Canadian Organic Growers' Association, is a network of growers dedicated to saving and exchanging seeds of heirloom varieties and endangered non-hybrid commercial varieties of vegetables, fruits, herbs, grains, forages and flowers. As people have stopped growing older varieties of plants, many have become extinct, resulting in the loss of our agricultural heritage and the genetic material necessary to ensure the continuity of our food supply.*

*When only a few strains of a particular crop are cultivated, farmers run the risk of seeing their entire crops devastated due to damage by insects and/or disease. For example, the Irish potato famine of 1848 is attributed to dependence on one variety, while Ceylon lost its position as the largest exporter of coffee because of rust, a common plant fungus.*

*Heritage varieties of vegetables, fruits, herbs and grains add richness and diversity to our lives. If you are interested in helping to ensure that these wonderful varieties will survive for the next generation to enjoy, please contact the Heritage Seed Program at R.R. #3, Uxbridge, Ontario, L9P 1R3.*

*Heather Apple's grandmother made this pie every year for her family's Thanksgiving dinner. Even though the family called it a pumpkin pie, Mrs. Apple always used hubbard squash (an heirloom squash still widely grown today), because of its richer flavour and texture. Most pumpkins are too watery and their flavour is poor compared to the hubbard. One exception to this is the white cheesequake pumpkin, a creamy-white heirloom variety that was the first pumpkin to be listed in a North American seed catalogue (1824).*

# Granny Apple's Pumpkin Pie

HEATHER APPLE, PRESIDENT
Heritage Seed Program
*Uxbridge, Ontario*

SERVES 8

| | | |
|---|---|---|
| 2 large or 3 small | eggs | 2 large or 3 small |
| 2 cups | puréed squash or pumpkin | 500 mL |
| 2 Tbsp | molasses | 25 mL |
| ¾ cup | brown sugar | 175 mL |
| 1½ cups | half and half (10%) cream | 375 mL |
| 1 tsp | cinnamon | 5 mL |
| ½ tsp | ginger | 2 mL |
| pinch | cloves | pinch |
| pinch | nutmeg | pinch |
| pinch | allspice | pinch |
| 1 | unbaked pie shell | 1 |

• Beat the eggs. Add other ingredients, mixing well, and pour into pieshell.
• Cook slowly in a moderate oven (about 325°–350°F/160°–180°C) anywhere from 1 hour and 20 minutes to 2 hours. Watch carefully. When a knife is inserted and comes out clean, the pie is finished. Cool before serving.

*One of the first to join the newly-formed Knives and Forks association, in the fall of 1989, Lorene Sauro has always had great energy and enthusiasm for the organization and the chef-grower relationship. As a commercial baker, Sauro took the initiative to support local farmers incorporating organic fruit and flour into her baking.*

# Peach and Blueberry Crumble Pie

LORENE SAURO
Cakes and Ayle Ltd.
*Concord, Ontario*

SERVES 8

***Pastry***

| | | |
|---|---|---|
| 1 | egg yolk | 1 |
| 2 Tbsp | water | 25 mL |
| 1 cup | soft organic white flour | 250 mL |
| ¾ cup | spelt flour | 175 mL |
| pinch | salt | pinch |
| 3 Tbsp | cold butter | 50 mL |
| 1 Tbsp | shortening | 15 mL |

***Crumble***

| | | |
|---|---|---|
| ½ cup | soft organic white flour | 125 mL |
| ½ cup | spelt flour | 125 mL |
| ⅓ cup | brown sugar | 75 mL |
| ¼ cup | cold butter | 50 mL |

***Filling***

| | | |
|---|---|---|
| 8 | medium peaches, sliced but not peeled | 8 |
| 1 cup | wild blueberries | 250 mL |
| 1 cup | brown sugar | 250 mL |
| 1 tsp | cinnamon | 5 mL |
| 2 Tbsp | cornstarch | 25 mL |

*Pastry*

• Mix water with egg yolk. Place flours, salt, butter and shortening in a food processor and process until butter is the size of small peas. Transfer to a bowl and add water mixture. Mix lightly with fingers until pastry holds together. Do not knead. (A pastry knife can also be used instead of a food processor.)

• Put ½ of the dough onto a lightly floured surface. Lightly flour a rolling pin. Roll pastry to a ¼-inch/.5-cm-thick circle. Fold in half and put in a 9-inch/22.5-cm pie plate. Unfold so that pastry is covering the entire inside surface of the pie plate and hanging over the edge by ½ inch. Fold overhang under so that there is a double thickness around the edge of the pie plate. Pinch pastry all around the edge with thumb and index finger. The other half of the pastry can be saved and frozen.

*Crumble*

• Process all ingredients in a food processor until crumbly or place in a bowl and cut with a pastry knife.

*Filling*

• Put fruit in a bowl. Mix sugar, cinnamon and cornstarch together. Mix with fruit.

• Pour fruit into pie shell. Sprinkle crumble on top.

• Bake at 400–425°F/200–220°C for 20 minutes. Lower oven temperature to 350°F/180°C and bake for 30 minutes more or until filling is cooked.

Tree-ripened peaches are best for this recipe. One early season variety, Brighton, is available from South Bay Vineyards at the Knives and Forks Market and is notable for its high concentration of flavour. Boker Organic Farms sells their spelt flour at the Barrie Farmers' Market (held at Barrie City Hall, Barrie, Ontario). They also sell it at their farm. Oak Manor Farms makes an excellent white flour, both soft and hard. All their flours are available at most health food stores. (*See Source Information at back of this book.*)

*Salmon berries are a small wild berry, sort of a cross between a raspberry and a blackberry. Their delicate flavour inspired John Rogers to create this unique parfait in which they are puréed and folded into a creamy white chocolate mousse. The results are sensational!*

# White Chocolate and Wild Salmon Berry Parfait

JOHN ROGERS
Windows on the Bay, Coast Plaza Hotel
*Vancouver, British Columbia*

SERVES 4

| | | |
|---|---|---|
| 1 cup | fresh wild salmon berries (if unavailable, substitute any fresh, organically-grown berries) | 250 mL |
| 1/4 cup | sugar | 50 mL |
| 5 oz | good-quality white chocolate | 150 g |
| 4 | egg yolks | 4 |
| 3/4 cup | 35% cream, whipped | 175 mL |
| 3 drops | vanilla extract | 3 drops |

- Purée the salmon berries and 2 Tbsp/25 mL of sugar in a food processor.
- Simmer the purée and reduce its volume to 1/3 cup/85 mL. Cool.
- Melt the white chocolate by simmering over hot water in a double boiler (or in a bowl of hot water).
- Mix together 1 oz/25 mL of the whipping cream, the remaining sugar, egg yolks and vanilla extract. Add the melted white chocolate to this custard mixture, and mix until cool.
- Whip remaining cream and fold into custard mixture.
- Into 1/3 of this mixture, fold in the salmon berry purée.

• Line a 6-inch x 4-inch x 2-inch/15-cm x 10-cm x 5-cm non-stick bread pan with plastic wrap.

• Alternate layers of both mixtures into lined mold and freeze overnight.

• Slice and serve with a few fresh berries and organic lemon balm.

The restaurant obtains the wild salmon berries from Glorious Garnishes in Aldergrove, British Columbia. (*See Source Information at back of book.*)

*My next door neighbour used to be in the fruit business, and every now and then he goes down to visit his buddies at the Ontario Food Terminal. He often returns with a few boxes of absolutely huge, perfect-looking strawberries. In his generous, neighbourly fashion, he usually drops off a box or two at our house, and my children immediately proceed to devour what they think are the most delicious strawberries they've ever eaten.*

*While I do appreciate his thoughtfulness, I can't help but wince a bit when I think of the chemicals that have been used to produce these impeccable specimens: Before planting, the soil is sprayed with various herbicides and nematocides, such as 2-4-D and Paraquat, which prevent the development of weeds and nematodes (a group of parasitic worms that live in the soil). While the plants are developing, such insecticides as Sevin, Captan, Malathion and Parathion, as well as various fungicides (Hyperex and Benelate being two of the more commonly known) are also applied. During their development, the plants are likely to be fertilized with water-soluble substances containing nitrites.*

*Does the average grocery shopper realize that by buying such produce we are merely perpetuating a system that is the largest single source of water pollution in North America?*

*Here are some facts and figures to ponder the next time you eye those perfect-looking strawberries in your neighborhood produce section: sixty-four percent of all impacted (moderately or severely polluted) rivers and fifty-seven percent of all impacted lakes are polluted by agricultural chemicals.* Chemical fertilizers such as nitrates and phosphates percolate throughout the soil and eventually find their way into the groundwater, and, in sufficient concentrations, can cause hypertension and methemoglobinemia (a condition in which the iron in the blood loses its capacity to bind with oxygen), and are also carcinogenic. The indiscriminate use of pesticides will usually kill whatever natural predators are living in the immediate environment, along with countless other victims, such as birds. (To say nothing of the increased incidence of cancer among those who manufacture, handle and apply pesticides.) And although pesticides may be developed to target specific pests, once in the water supply their toxicity is no longer selective, and they persist in the environment, some for longer* *than five years. Thus, their dangers become magnified the higher you go in the food chain.*

*The organic grower, on the other hand, begins the year before by planting a green manure crop such as oil radish, which, when worked into the soil the following spring, acts to naturally suppress nematodes. Composted horse manure is also applied to help achieve a high level of organic material in the soil. The subsoil is turned to prevent compaction, and thus discourage the growth of weeds. Ken and Martha Laing, who cultivate two acres of strawberries just south of London, Ontario, rotate the acreage under cultivation each year. Each two-acre plot is cultivated only once every three years, which also helps inhibit weed growth. "We cultivate and hoe all the weeds by hand," says Mrs. Laing, adding, "It is, by far, the mostly costly, most labour-intensive aspect of our production."*

*The Laings switched from conventional to organic strawberry production out of a concern for the environment and for their own health. They also say there has been a "change in public sentiment in recent years — there is definitely more interest in organically-raised produce today." For the most part, pests and fungi have not been a problem, according to Mrs. Laing, because, "When you have healthy soil you have healthy plants."*

*Less than fifty years ago people could eat either locally-grown food in season or foods that had been preserved by drying or canning. Today, we must deal with not only the inferior taste and quality of out-of-season produce from distant sources, but the environmental impact of consuming them as well. That impact also includes the pollution caused by transporting them by ground across entire continents.*

*In our northern climate do we really need strawberries in the middle of January for sustenance? A simple poached pear or apple tart would be much more seasonally appropriate and perhaps even more satisfying.*

*This wonderful dessert, created by Bryan Steele of The Old Prune in Stratford, is meant to be enjoyed at that one perfect moment in June when, after craving strawberries for nearly a year, they finally arrive, and there is still some rhubarb left in the garden.*

* Brown, Lester, *State of the World 1987*, W.W. Norton & Co., 1987.

# Orange-Rhubarb Cake with Vanilla Cream and Fresh Strawberries

BRYAN STEELE
The Old Prune
*Stratford, Ontario*

SERVES 4

***Cake***

| | | |
|---|---|---|
| ¾ lb | rhubarb, washed, peeled, and cut into ½-inch/1-cm pieces | 300 g |
| ½ cup | slivered almonds, toasted | 125 mL |
| ½ cup | candied orange peel | 125 mL |
| splash | Grand Marnier liqueur | splash |
| 1 | vanilla bean | 1 |
| 2 cups | whipping cream | 500 mL |
| ½ cup | sugar | 125 mL |
| 7 | eggs, beaten | 7 |
| ¾ lb | sponge cake or brioche (preferably 1 day old) cut into 1-inch/2.5-cm pieces | 300 g |

***Vanilla Cream***

| | | |
|---|---|---|
| 2 | vanilla beans | 2 |
| 1 cup | 35% whipping cream | 250 mL |
| 1 cup | milk | 250 mL |
| ½ cup | sugar | 125 mL |
| 5 | egg yolks | 5 |
| ½ cup | 35% cream, whipped | 125 mL |
| | | |
| 2 cups | strawberries, washed and hulled | 500 mL |

### *Vanilla Cream*

• Using a paring knife, split the vanilla beans lengthwise and scrape the seeds away from the inside of the pods into a saucepan containing the whipping cream and milk. Bring this to a boil over medium heat, watching carefully so that the milk does not boil over.

• Remove from the heat and stir in the sugar. Cover and let this mixture steep for 30 minutes.

• Beat the egg yolks to a creamy texture and add some of the hot mixture to them. Stir well and then combine the egg yolks into the heated milk and cream.

• Return to a low heat and stir continually, until the mixture coats the back of a wooden spoon. Remove from the heat and chill until cold. Fold in the whipped cream and refrigerate.

### *Cake*

• In a large mixing bowl, combine the rhubarb with the almonds, orange peel and Grand Marnier. Let stand to marinate for 1–2 hours before proceeding with the recipe.

• Remove the seeds from the vanilla bean as for the vanilla cream and scrape into a second bowl. Add the cream, sugar and beaten eggs. Using a whisk, beat this mixture until well combined. Add to the marinated rhubarb and orange peel. Preheat oven to 425°F/220°C. Add the cake cubes, mix well again and pour the entire mixture into a 10-inch/22–24-cm square buttered baking dish with sides that are a minimum of 1½ inch/3 cm high.

• Bake for 25 to 30 minutes. Cake is done when a skewer or toothpick inserted into the centre comes out clean. Cool. Using a round or fluted cookie cutter, 4 inches/8 cm in diameter, cut into individual cakes.

### *To serve*

• Reheat the individual cakes on a nonstick baking sheet in a hot, 450°F/230°C oven for 5 minutes. Spoon the chilled vanilla cream onto a dessert plate, place the cake in the centre and garnish with fresh strawberries.

In Ontario, certified growers Ken and Martha Laing of St. Thomas and Rainbow Hills in Chatsworth offer pick-your-own and ready-picked strawberries. (*See Source Information at back of book.*)

*When offered a dish in which flowers are used as garnish, or even as part of the main dish, many of us might recoil at first. Eating flowers is simply not a part of our culinary heritage, and yet, in many other cultures, both ancient and modern, people grow up eating flowers without giving it a second thought. Today, edible flowers are gaining popularity as cooks discover their potential to add flavour as well as aesthetically enhance a variety of dishes. Sooke Harbour House in British Columbia, whose magnificent kitchen gardens contain roughly thirty-five different varieties of edible flowers (and more than 350 varieties of herbs, vegetables and fruits), is an innovator in the use of edible flowers and unusual plants.*

*If you have never attempted to cook with flowers before, do not be intimidated by this recipe; it is nothing more than a traditional baked custard flavoured with anise hyssop flowers. This herbaceous ornamental perennial has gray-green leaves and striking, dense, 1–2 inch/2–4 cm flowers, ranging from mauve to lavender. The petals have a slight anise–root beer flavour and are often used in soups, salads, desserts and flavoured butters. If anise hyssop is not available, don't be afraid to experiment with other types of edible flowers, such as violets, lavender, roses or even apple blossoms. You may even want to consider planting your own edible flower garden next spring!*

*This custard dessert was created for Sooke Harbour House by David Feys, who has cooked there since 1989. A graduate of George Brown College, David has also worked at The Windsor Arms and Nekah.*

# Anise Hyssop Flower Custard with Black Pansy Syrup and Gooseberry Purée

DAVID FEYS
Sooke Harbour House
*Sooke, British Columbia*

SERVES 6

| | | |
|---|---|---|
| 1 cup | homogenized milk | 250 mL |
| 1 cup | 35% cream | 250 mL |
| ¼ cup | white sugar | 50 mL |
| 6 Tbsp | anise hyssop flowers | 90 mL |
| 2 | large eggs | 2 |
| 3 | large egg yolks | 3 |

***Garnish***

| | | |
|---|---|---|
| 2 cups | black pansy syrup (recipe follows) | 500 mL |
| 2 Tbsp | anise hyssop flowers | 25 mL |
| 6 | anise hyssop leaves | 6 |
| 6 | black pansy flowers | 6 |
| ½ cup | red english gooseberry purée (recipe follows) | 125 mL |
| 12 | red english gooseberries | 12 |

• Combine milk and cream. Put half of this mixture into a small saucepan with sugar and the anise hyssop flowers. Scald the mixture on low heat. Remove from heat and add remaining milk mixture. Stir well and set aside to cool. Cover and refrigerate overnight, if possible. The length of time allotted to letting the anise hyssop steep in this mixture will greatly affect the finished product.

• Preheat oven to 350°F/180°C. Fill a 9 x 13-inch/23 x 32.5-cm Pyrex or aluminum pan with enough hot water to reach halfway up the sides of six 4-oz/125-mL custard molds. Put this prepared *bain marie* into the oven.

• In a medium-sized bowl, beat the eggs and egg yolks well. Strain the flowers and add the cooled infused milk mixture to the beaten eggs and egg yolks. Combine well and pour equal amounts into 6 clean, dry custard molds.

• Bake in the *bain marie* for 25 to 30 minutes. To test for doneness, insert a small knife into the centre of a custard. If clean when removed, it is properly cooked.

• Use a pair of tongs to remove custard molds from the *bain marie* to a cooling rack. Allow to cool completely and refrigerate for at least 1 hour. Then remove by running a small knife around the edge of the mold and invert directly onto a serving plate.

• *Presentation*: Invert custard onto a plate. Arrange gooseberry purée in a circular fashion around the plate near the custard to contain the black pansy syrup. Pour the syrup over top. Decorate each plate with 1 tsp/5 mL of anise hyssop flowers, 1 anise hyssop leaf, a black pansy flower and 4 red english gooseberry halves.

## *Black Pansy Syrup*

MAKES 2 CUPS

| | | |
|---|---|---|
| 2 cups | white sugar | 500 mL |
| 1 cup | water | 250 mL |
| 1 cup | black pansy petals | 250 mL |

• Clean pansies and shake off excess water. Pull petals from green stems. Put pansy petals into a food processor fitted with a steel blade and add ⅓ cup/75 mL sugar. Grind pansies into sugar using 4 pulses. Then process for about 30 seconds.

• Combine sugar, pansy/sugar mixture and water in a small saucepan. Over medium heat, bring the mixture to a boil. Stir once and reduce the heat to low. Allow to simmer and cook to syrup stage. If you have one, use a candy thermometer and do not exceed 220°F/110°C. When the mixture reaches syrup stage, remove it from the heat and pour into a heat-proof container. Allow to cool.

### *Red English Gooseberry Purée*

| | | |
|---|---|---|
| 3 cups | red english gooseberries | 750 mL |
| to taste | maple syrup (optional) | to taste |

• In a food processor fitted with a steel blade, purée the gooseberries. Sieve through a medium-meshed strainer. If desired, sweeten with maple syrup, to taste.
• Use 1–1½ Tbsp/15–20 mL per serving as a garnish for the Anise Hyssop Flower Custard.

*In June 1992, one of this country's most talented, most lauded chefs, Jamie Kennedy, returned to his familiar post behind the stoves of Palmerston, his landmark restaurant at the corner of Toronto's College and Bathurst Streets, where he renewed his quest for "a Canadian identity in food culture."*

*One of the most dedicated advocates of seasonal cooking, Kennedy possesses a gift for celebrating the most ordinary of locally-grown ingredients. "We live in a time when everything is available to us year round," says Kennedy. "A true cook should be able to use cooking skills to create based on what is available locally." With partner Marcel Rethoré at the helm, Kennedy is ebullient about the new, simpler Palmerston. "I've always wanted the chance to reach as many people as possible," he says. Today, Jamie Kennedy remains an outspoken proponent of organically-grown ingredients, and the effort he has expended in order to elevate public taste and our connection with the land puts him in a class by himself.*

*Jamie Kennedy created this recipe for A Celebration of Canadian Cuisine, a benefit for the Stratford Chefs School, which was held at Toronto's Centro restaurant on March 1, 1992. Joining him on this occasion were Sinclair Philip and David Feys of Sooke Harbour House and Serge Bruyère of À la Table de Serge Bruyère, who each prepared a different course. Although this dessert requires a number of steps before the final assembly, they can all be done in advance.*

# Warm Apple Cake with Ontario Fruit and Maple Ice Cream

JAMIE KENNEDY
Palmerston Restaurant
*Toronto, Ontario*

SERVES 6

***Apple Purée***

| | | |
|---|---|---|
| 2½ | spy or spartan apples | 2½ |
| ¼ cup | apple cider | 50 mL |
| | juice of ½ lemon | |

• Roughly chop apples without peeling or coring. Place them in a stainless steel saucepan. Add lemon juice, cider and cover. Place saucepan on low heat and simmer until very tender (approximately 10 minutes.)
• Purée in a food processor and then pass through a fine sieve. Reserve.

***Cake***

| | | |
|---|---|---|
| 4 | eggs | 4 |
| ⅔ cup | sugar | 150 mL |
| 5 Tbsp | melted butter | 75 mL |
| ½ cup | apple purée | 125 mL |
| 1 cup | pastry flour | 250 mL |

• Mix eggs and sugar in a large stainless steel bowl. Whisk vigorously with a wire whisk for approximately 10 minutes. Sift pastry flour and fold into the egg mixture alternately with the apple purée. Fold melted butter into batter. Transfer to greased loaf pan.
• Bake in a preheated 350°F/180°C oven for approximately 45 minutes, until golden brown. Cool and remove from pan.

### *Maple Tuile*

| | | |
|---|---|---|
| ½ Tbsp | maple syrup | 7 mL |
| 2 Tbsp | sugar | 25 mL |
| 2 Tbsp | unsalted butter, softened | 25 mL |
| 2 | egg whites | 2 |
| ½ cup | flour | 125 mL |

• Combine maple syrup and sugar in a stainless steel bowl. Cream together with the butter until light. Alternately add the egg whites and the sifted pastry flour until all are incorporated into mix. Refrigerate 2 hours prior to using.
• Fashion a maple leaf template using a plastic lid and an exacto knife. (The template is the shape of the leaf cut out of the lid — like a stencil.) Grease the back of a cookie sheet with butter and place template on it.
• Spread tuile batter over the surface of the maple leaf shape. Lift template and repeat until cookie sheet is full of of maple leaf shaped cookies.
• Bake in 375°F/190°C oven for approximately 5 minutes. While still warm, remove from pan and drape over shallow cup to simulate leaf form and to cool.
• Store in a covered tin until ready to serve.

### *Cider Glaze*

| | | |
|---|---|---|
| 2 cups | apple cider | 500 mL |

• Place cider in an uncovered, stainless steel saucepan. Simmer at boiling until volume of cider is reduced by ⅔. (Yielding 1⅓ cups reduced cider). Reserve.

### *Maple Ice Cream*

| | | |
|---|---|---|
| 1 | vanilla bean | 1 |
| 1 cup | milk | 250 mL |
| 1 cup | 35% cream | 250 mL |
| 2 Tbsp | *crème fraîche* (see recipe on page 163) | 25 mL |
| 6 | egg yolks | 6 |
| ¾ cup | maple syrup | 175 mL |

• Split vanilla bean in half lengthwise and scrape out the paste.
• Scald milk and cream in a stainless steel saucepan.
• Meanwhile, place *crème fraîche* in a 1-quart/4-litre container. Place a sieve or conical strainer over container.
• Combine egg yolks and maple syrup in a stainless steel bowl. When milk is scalding, remove from heat. Add some of the milk to the egg yolk mixture. Return egg yolk mixture to saucepan with milk. Slowly heat egg yolk and milk mixture to make a custard, stirring constantly. When thick, pour through strainer into *crème fraîche* to cool. Stir in the scrapings from the vanilla bean.
• When cool, chill in an ice cream maker according to manufacturer's directions. Store in freezer until read to use.

### *Riesling poached pears*

| | | |
|---|---|---|
| 1 | bottle riesling wine | 1 |
| ¼ cup | sugar | 50 mL |
| 2 | bosc pears | 2 |
| 1 | vanilla bean | 1 |

• Place riesling and sugar in an uncovered saucepan and reduce by ⅔. Add vanilla bean and whole, unpeeled, uncored pears. Simmer, covered, turning periodically, until pears are soft.
• Cool pears in cooking liquid and reserve until ready to serve.

### *Pinot Noir Glaze*

| | | |
|---|---|---|
| 1 | bottle pinot noir wine | 1 |
| ¼ cup | sugar | 50 mL |
| 2 Tbsp | butter | 25 mL |

• Place pinot noir and sugar in an uncovered saucepan. Reduce until syrupy. Cut butter into small cubes and whisk into wine syrup. Reserve.

### *Final Assembly and Presentation*

• Slice cake into 6 equal slices and place them on a baking sheet. Soak each slice thoroughly with cider glaze.
• Slice pears in half lengthwise and then slice each half into thin slices. Reserve juice in small pitcher.

• Lay out 6 dinner-size plates. Place a dollop of apple purée in the centre of each plate. Pour a thin bean of pinot noir glaze around the perimeter of apple purée. Place a slice of soaked apple cake on the purée.

• Place two "fans" of sliced pears on either side of apple cake. Drizzle reserved poaching liquid over pears.

• Place one maple tuile directly above the apple cake. Place one large scoop of ice cream on the maple tuile. Serve immediately.

*Lorene Sauro was producing desserts and prepared foods for Fitz-Henri Fine Foods in Toronto when her brother mentioned that he was looking to make a career change. "If you bake it, I'll sell it," he said and Cakes and Ayle was born. When Lorene announced that she was leaving her job, John Fitz-Henri promptly signed up as her first customer, and has remained steadfastly loyal ever since. Today, Cakes and Ayle Ltd. supplies a complete line of fresh and frozen fancy cakes, pies, squares and mousses to stores, restaurants and distributors throughout Ontario.*

*In a competitive industry where many commercial bakeries mix their cream with non-dairy creamer and their butter with margarine, Lorene ensures a high standard of quality that begins with the finest ingredients. "Our icings are all butter," she asserts. "We use fresh cream, fine Belgian chocolate, and our flour is one hundred percent organic. The organic flour really produces a better product — I can even taste the difference."*

# Chocolate Cream Gratin with Wild Thimbleberries

LORENE SAURO
Cakes and Ayle Ltd.
*Concord, Ontario*

SERVES 6

**Crust**

| | | |
|---|---|---|
| 3 Tbsp | unsalted butter, cold | 50 mL |
| ¾ cup | hard organic white flour | 175 mL |
| 1 Tbsp | cocoa | 15 mL |
| ¼ cup | brown sugar | 50 mL |
| ¼ cup | chopped filberts | 50 mL |
| 1 oz | bittersweet or semi-sweet chocolate, chopped | 30 g |

*Cream Gratin*

| | | |
|---|---|---|
| 4 | egg yolks | 4 |
| ¼ cup | brown sugar | 50 mL |
| 1 cup | whipping cream | 250 mL |
| dash | vanilla | dash |
| ½–1 oz | (depending on how chocolatey you like it) good-quality semi-sweet, chocolate, melted | 15–30 g |
| ½ cup | wild thimbleberries | 125 mL |
| pinch | sugar | pinch |

### *Crust*

• Place butter, flour, cocoa and sugar in a processor and process until crumbly. Add nuts and gently pulse to mix. Or, place butter, sugar, flour and cocoa in a bowl. Cut with a pastry knife until crumbly. Mix in nuts.

• Press into 6 individual ramekins or tart pans. An 8-inch/20-cm gratin dish can also be used. Bake at 350°F/180°C for 20 minutes.

• Remove from oven and place 1/6 of the chocolate in each dish. When the heat of the crust has melted the chocolate, spread it over the surface of the crust with a rubber spatula. Let cool until chocolate is hard.

### *Cream Gratin*

• If berries are very tart, sprinkle with a pinch of sugar. Place egg yolks and brown sugar in a bowl over a pot with hot water in it and whisk until slightly thickened and light yellow in colour.

• Transfer pot to the stove and, over simmering water, add cream and whisk until temperature of mixture is hot to the touch. Remove from the stove.

• Carefully fold in the vanilla and melted chocolate.

• Transfer to a mixer and beat until cool (about 10 minutes). This can all be done up to 3 hours ahead.

### *Final assembly*

• Sprinkle berries over crust. Pour cream mixture over berries and bake at 350°F/180°C for 15–20 minutes or until custard is firm but still jiggly. Serve warm.

*Note:* It is very important that the berries be full of flavour so that their taste is not overwhelmed by the chocolate. Fruits such as raspberries, strawberries, peaches or other favourites may also be substituted.

Thimbleberries, more commonly known as blackberries, can often be found growing wild on the borders of woodlands and fields. They are shaped like a "thimble" and when picked ripe are very juicy and flavourful. Available from Cookstown Greens — in season — and at the Knives and Forks Organic Market in Toronto. (*See Source Information at back of book.*)

*Tucked away in the small town of Bloomfield, Austrian-born Willy Fida draws upon a well-developed network of local farmers, several of whom practice organic methods, and fifteen of the area's commercial fisherman to supply him with ingredients for his historic restaurant, Angeline's. "We really try to use as many locally-grown, seasonal products as possible," says Fida. "It gives one a better sense of the seasons." Fida harvests rhubarb from his own garden for this strudel, a luscious conclusion to any springtime menu.*

*Angeline's serves locally-caught yellow perch and pickerel from May to June, frogs' legs in August and whitefish in the fall. In the summer, Fida obtains peppers in a rainbow of colours, Oriental eggplants and heritage varieties of cucumbers and tomatoes from local organic grower Phil Mathewson, who also sells his produce at the weekly Knives and Forks Organic Market.*

# Rhubarb Strudel with an Almond Sauce

WILLY FIDA
Angeline's Restaurant
*Bloomfield, Ontario*

SERVES 10–15

### *Dough*

| | | |
|---|---|---|
| 1¾ cups | pastry flour | 425 mL |
| 4 tsp | vegetable oil | 20 mL |
| ½ tsp | salt | 2 mL |
| ⅓ cup | lukewarm water | 75 mL |
| | | |
| ½ cup | melted butter | 125 mL |

### *Butter Crumbs*

| | | |
|---|---|---|
| ½ cup | unsalted butter | 125 mL |
| 2 Tbsp | white sugar | 25 mL |

| | | |
|---|---|---|
| 1 tsp | vanilla sugar | 5 mL |
| 1 tsp | ground cinnamon | 5 mL |
| 1 cup | white bread crumbs | 250 mL |

***Filling***

| | | |
|---|---|---|
| 2¼ lbs | young rhubarb | 1 kg |
| 1 cup | brown sugar | 250 mL |
| ½ cup | raisins | 125 mL |
| to taste | cinnamon | to taste |
| ¾ cup | ground almonds (toasted if desired) | 175 mL |

***Almond Sauce***

| | | |
|---|---|---|
| 1 cup | milk | 250 mL |
| ¼ cup | sugar | 50 mL |
| 1 Tbsp | vanilla sugar | 15 mL |
| | salt | |
| 1 Tbsp | cornstarch | 15 mL |
| 1 | egg yolk | 1 |

• Prepare strudel dough by placing flour in mixing bowl. Add vegetable oil, salt, water and beat dough with an electric mixer for about 10 minutes until it is smooth and elastic. Form the dough into a ball. Set in a mixing bowl in which you have sprinkled some sifted flour, then sprinkle the ball of dough with a bit more flour. Cover the dough with plastic wrap and let it rest for about half an hour at room temperature.

• Meanwhile, prepare the butter crumbs. Melt the ½ cup/125 mL of butter in a small saucepan over medium heat. Add the white sugar, vanilla sugar, and cinnamon. Warm the mixture carefully over low heat. Stir in the bread crumbs and simmer very gently for 2 minutes.

***Filling***

• Select only the younger stalks (the bigger ones are woody and stringy and not good for strudel). Peel them with a knife and cut into ½-inch/1½-cm lengths. Place rhubarb pieces in a mixing bowl, then add the brown sugar, raisins, cinnamon and ground almonds. Gently mix ingredients together.

• Take the strudel dough and place it on a piece of floured pastry cloth, approximately 3 feet x 3 feet/ 90 cm x 90 cm. Sprinkle some flour on the dough again and start to roll it out as thin as you possibly can. Then start pulling the dough very carefully with your hands, until you obtain a very thin square shape, approximately 2 feet x 2 feet/60 cm x 60 cm.

• Carefully brush some melted butter on all 4 ends. Spread the butter crumbs on the dough, leaving a 1-inch/2.5-cm border uncovered the whole way around. Spread the rhubarb filling over the crumbs. Preheat the oven to 350°F/180°C.

• Grasp the 2 top ends of the cloth and roll the dough towards you to form a strudel. Holding the ends of the cloth, lift the strudel up and place it on a baking sheet, making sure the ends are tucked in. Brush the strudel with melted butter and bake for 15 minutes, then lower the heat to 300°F/150°C and continue baking for approximately 30 minutes more. Remove from the oven and brush once or twice again with melted butter. Let the strudel rest for 15 minutes.

### *Almond Sauce*

• Heat milk to just below boiling. Add sugar, vanilla sugar, and a pinch of salt. In a separate bowl, mix cornstarch with egg yolk and a spoonful of milk. Bring milk and sugar mixture to a boil and whisk in cornstarch-egg yolk mixture. Remove from heat. Flavour to taste with some almond liqueur, if desired.

• Sprinkle strudel with icing sugar to finish. Serve with warm sauce.

# Source Information

The following is a list of selected retailers across Canada who sell organically grown foods, as well as information on sources mentioned in this book. Please note: some of these sources may not sell to the public. For a more extensive list of certified organic growers, wholesalers, associations, etc. in Canada consult the *Directory of Organic Agriculture*, published by Canadian Organic Growers, Box 6408, Station J, Ottawa, ONT K2A 3Y6.

**BRITISH COLUMBIA**

Arbutus Deer Farms
Mayne Island, B.C.
V0N 2J0
(604) 539-2301

Fallow deer, pheasant and sheep for sale to restaurants. Local direct sales.

Gary Argyle
2403 Maxey Road
Nanaimo, B.C. V9R 5K3
(604) 754-9272

Organic grower of seasonal vegetables.

Capers
2496 Marine Drive
W. Vancouver, B.C.
V7V 1L1
(604) 925-3316

Large whole foods store with emphasis on a wide variety of organic foods. In-store restaurant and deli.

Cedar Creek Winery
c/o Grady Wine
Marketing Inc.
3134 E. 20th Avenue
Vancouver, B.C. V5M 2V5
(604) 433-1091

Distributor of Cedar Creek Wines.

| | |
|---|---|
| Granville Island Public Market<br>1440 Johnson Street<br>Vancouver B.C. V6H 1S1<br>(604) 666-5784 | Open 7 days a week, 9 a.m.–6 p.m., closed Mondays, Thanksgiving, Victoria Day. |
| Hazelmere Farm<br>1831–184th Street<br>Surrey, B.C. V38 5G9<br>(604) 538-3018 | Diversified farm with wide range of vegetables, berries, and herbs. Farm stand. Restaurant, retail sales. |
| Hazelwood Herb Farm<br>R.R. #1<br>Ladysmith, B.C.<br>V0R 2E0<br>(604) 245-8007 | Fresh herbs in season. |
| Hills Foods Ltd.<br>3650 Bonneville Place, Suite 109<br>Burnaby, B.C. V3N 4T7<br>(604) 421-3100 | Distributor of specialty meats, produce, and gourmet items. Over-the-counter sales of selected items to the public. |
| Horizon Distributors, a division of C.R.S. Worker's Co-op<br>8335 Winston Street<br>Burnaby, B. C. V5A 2H3<br>(604) 420-6751 | Distributor of natural and organically-grown foods, bulk and packaged items to manufacturers, retailers, restaurants and co-ops. |
| Ernie Knott<br>4810 Sooke Road<br>Sooke, B.C. V0S 1N0<br>(604) 642-5120 | Seasonal vegetables and fruit: lettuce, peas, beets, carrots, broad beans, red english goose-berries, tayberries. Farm stand. |
| Kootenay Country Store Co-Operative<br>295 Baker Street<br>Nelson, B.C. V1L 4H4<br>(604) 354-4077 | Natural and organic foods retailer. |

Omega Nutrition
8392 Prince Edward Street
Vancouver, B.C. V5X 3R9
(604) 322-8862

Manufacturer of certified organic fresh-pressed, unrefined oils.

Rodear Meats
Box 15
Big Lake, B.C. V0L 1G0
(604) 243-2340

Processor of organically-raised beef from Rafter K Ranch. Sells to restaurants and the public.

The Glorious Garnish and Seasonal Salad Company
374–256th Street
Aldergrove, B.C. V0X 1A0
(604) 851-1400

Grower and supplier of unusual produce to B.C. restaurants. Sells to the public at the Granville Island Market.

Yellow Island Aquaculture
1681 Brook Crescent
Campbell River, B.C.
V9W 6K9
(604) 923-5823

Salmon farm producing organically-raised salmon from its own stock. Sells to restaurants, retailers and individuals in Vancouver–Victoria–Nanaimo area.

**ALBERTA**

Community Natural Foods
1403–10 Avenue SW
Calgary, AB T3C 3R4
(403) 229-2383

Health and natural foods retailer, featuring organic produce, grains and flours.

Nutter's Fruit and Nut Co. Ltd.
107–1601 Dunmore Road SE
Medicine Hat, AB
T1A 1Z8
(403) 529-1664

Twenty-seven stores across western Canada including Red Deer, Lethbridge, Jasper, Swift Current and Brandon.

## SASKATCHEWAN

Healthy Harvest Food and Craft Co-op Ltd.
Box 1856
Tisdale, SK S0E 1T0
(306) 873-4685

Non-profit, whole foods co-operative with emphasis on organic, locally-grown foods. Organic grains, beans, meats and produce.

## MANITOBA

Harvest Collective
877 Westminster Avenue
Winnipeg, MB R3G 1B3
(204) 772-4359

Retail store featuring grains, flours, packaged goods, eggs, and organically-grown produce. (Larger, locally-grown selection in season).

Nutter's Natural Foods
565–34 Street
Sunset Village,
Brandon, MB R7B 3P8
(204) 772-4359

Flours, grains, beans, packaged goods. Seasonal fruits and vegetables.

## ONTARIO

Alternatives Natural Food Market
880 Upper Wentworth
Hamilton, ONT L9A 5H2
(416) 388-8400

Full line of natural and organic products including fresh produce, meat, seafood, groceries and baked goods.

Alternatives Natural Food Market
579 Kerr Street
Oakville, ONT L6K 3E1
(416) 844-2375

Full line of natural and organic products including fresh produce, meat, seafood, groceries and baked goods.

Francis D. Avernis
R.R. #5
Stratford, ONT N5A 6S6
(519) 273-1672

Raspberries, blackberries, red and black currants; herbs. Restaurants and direct sales.

| | |
|---|---|
| Baldwin Natural Foods<br>20½ Baldwin Street<br>Toronto, ONT M5T 1L2<br>(416) 979-1777 | Organic dried beans, dried vegetables, grains. |
| Larry Bender<br>R.R. #2<br>Tavistock, ONT N0B 2R0<br>(519) 655-2082 | Lamb, beef, pork, chicken, turkey, maple syrup. |
| Bioharvest<br>1734 Trinity Road<br>R.R. #2<br>Ancaster, ONT L9G 3L1<br>(416) 648-0931 | Grower of specialty mushrooms for sale to restaurants. |
| Black River Game Farm<br>7171 R.R. #1<br>Pefferlaw, ONT L0E 1N0<br>(416) 722-6091 | Producer/distributor of game birds and grain-fed, free range chicken for sale to restaurants. |
| Boker Organic Farms<br>R.R. #3<br>Elmvale, ONT L0L 1P0<br>(705) 322-1189 | Demeter-certified producer of spelt, oats and rye. Red Wattle pork and Beefalo (freezer orders). |
| Burgess and Martin Organic Farms<br>R.R. #1<br>Harrow, ONT N0R 1G0<br>(519) 738-3995 | Culinary herbs and gourmet vegetables for sale to restaurants. |
| Community of the Brethren<br>R. R. #5<br>Bright, ONT N0J 1B0<br>(519) 684-7309 | Free range geese and goose fat by the pail. |

Cookstown Greens
P.O. Box 227
Cookstown, ONT
L0L 1L0
(705) 458-9077

Grower-distributor of specialty produce including unique mix of baby salad greens, edible flowers, French filet beans, multi-coloured tomatoes, potatoes, beets and carrots.

Cream of the Crop
345 Erb Street
Waterloo, ONT N2L 1W4
(519) 725-3378

Specialty produce store featuring organic produce from Burgess and Martin and other local organic growers in season.

Creative Hands Enterprises (Kingview Farms)
Box 366
Aurora, ONT L4G 3L5
(416) 727-3654

Certified grower and distributor of organic produce. Hydroponic salad greens.

Encounter Farm Enterprises
R.R. #1
Southwold, ONT N0L 2G0
(519) 764-2318

Specialty vegetables, i.e., baby squash, baby carrots, edible flowers. Restaurants, food stores and some direct sales.

Filsinger Natural Foods and Orchards Retail Store
R.R. #3
Ayton, ONT N0G 1C0
(519) 665-7763

Growers, wholesalers and retailers of apples, apple products and other food products.

Full Circle Foods
346 King Street W.
Kitchener, ONT N2G 1B7
(519) 744-5331

Wide variety of organic and natural foods including produce, flours, coffee, dried fruits and nuts.

Grains and Beans Ltd.
368 Piccadilly Street
London, ONT N6A 1S4
(519) 679-1001

Natural food store established in 1974.

| | |
|---|---|
| Greyburr Farm<br>R.R. #4<br>Markdale, ONT N0C 1H0<br>(519) 986-2672 | Asparagus, rhubarb and herbs from May until end of harvest. Retail store on the farm. |
| Ernie Hacquoil<br>R.R. #3<br>1825 Kamview Road<br>Thunder Bay, ONT<br>P7C 4V2<br>(807) 475-7552 | Fiddleheads. |
| Harmony Whole Foods<br>10 First Street<br>Orangeville, ONT<br>L9W 2C4<br>(519) 941-8961 | Fresh organic produce and a large selection of packaged organic foods. |
| Highland Springs Trout Farm<br>Walters Falls, ONT<br>N0H 2S0<br>(519) 538-3175 | O.C.I.A.-certified trout farm. Whole fish, smoked and Fresh fillets. Direct to health food stores and restaurants, St. Lawrence, Knives and Forks markets. |
| Ted Horychuk<br>R.R. #1<br>1917 22nd Side Road<br>Thunder Bay, ONT<br>P7C 4T9<br>(807) 939-2830 | Salad greens, Italian garlic. |
| Ivanhoe Gardens<br>R.R. #5<br>Madoc, ONT K0K 2K0<br>(613) 395-3719 | Organic grower specializing in garlic, shallots, fresh and potted herbs for sale to restaurants and retail outlets |

Knives and Forks
Organic Market
Movenpick Restaurant
165 York Street
Toronto, ONT M5H 3R8
(416) 366-8986

Organic farmers market held on Saturdays, from 8 a.m.–1:30 p.m. For further information please address all correspondence and inquiries to:
Ms. Antonita Chan
273 Claremont Street
2nd Floor
Toronto, ONT M6J 2N1
(416) 532-3997

Ken and Martha Laing
R.R.#5
St. Thomas, ONT N5P 3S8
(519) 775-2789

Pick-your-own and ready-picked strawberries. Raspberries and peaches in season.

Natural Food Market
92 Lodge Street
Waterloo, ONT N2J 2V6
(519) 884-1811

Retail store with an emphasis on organic products.

Noah's Natural Foods
322 Bloor Street W
Toronto, ONT M5S 1W5
(416) 968-7930

Wide selection of organic produce, bulk and natural foods

North Ridge Turkey Farm
R.R. # 1
Essex, ONT N8M 2X5
(519) 839-4198

Free range, non-medicated turkeys and turkey products.

Oak Manor Farms
R.R. #1
Tavistock, ONT N0B 2R0
(519) 662-2385

Processors of certified organic grains. Products are available at natural foods stores.

Oishi Mushrooms
1730 Hoxton Street
Claremont, ONT L0H 1E0
(416) 649-2343

Wholesaler of specialty mushrooms and herbs.

Organic Quack
R.R. #2
Mitchell, ONT N0K 1N0
(519) 393-5238

Certified free range muscovy and mallard ducks.

Ottawa Farmers Market
Kingview United Church
630 Island Park Drive
Ottawa, ONT K1Y 0B7

Operates every Saturday from 10 a.m. – 2 p.m.

Robert Passmore
R.R. #3
St. Mary's, ONT N0M 2V0
(519) 284-1459

Organic beef and chickens. Restaurants, farm gate sales.

Poplar Lane Farm
R.R. #4
Alliston, ONT L0M 1A0
(705) 435-5610

Lamb, free-run eggs and seasonal vegetables, including lettuces, potatoes, tomatoes, garlic and jerusalem artichokes.

Pusateri's Fine Foods
1539 Avenue Road
Toronto, ONT M5M 3X4
(416) 785-9100

Gourmet grocery store featuring selected organic items. Produce and packaged goods.

Rainbow Hills
R.R. #1
Chatsworth, ONT
N0H 1G0
(519) 794-3159

Pick-your-own and ready-picked strawberries and seasonal vegetables. Beef, pork, chickens, geese and eggs.

Ken Rogers
R.R. #5
Mount Forest, ONT
N0G 2L0
(519) 323-4935

Rabbits, wild turkeys, and free range eggs.

Roth Family Farms
R.R. #4
Picton, ONT K0K 2T0
(613) 476-5097

Producer of O.C.I.A.-certified chicken.

Rowe Farm Meats
R.R. #4
Guelph, ONT
N1H 6J1
(519) 822-8794

Beef, pork, chicken, lamb and deli meats from animals raised without growth promotants and subtherapeutic antibiotics. MSG and lactose-free deli meats.

South Bay Vineyards
R.R.#2
Milford, ONT
K0K 2P0
(613) 476-3750

O.C.I.A.-certified grower of wide range of heirloom fruits and vegetables. More than 100 varieties of grapes on developing vineyard and winery. Cider and fresh-pressed juices.

Stickling's Landhaus Bakery
R.R. #5
Peterborough, ONT
K9J 6X6
(705) 741-0777

Baker of tasty, wholesome, and healthful breads made from freshly ground organic grain.

Tara Natural Foods
340 King Street E
Kingston, ONT K7L 3B6
(613) 546-4439

Wide selection of organic and health foods.

The Apple Barn
R.R. #1
Brownsville, ONT
N0L 1C0
(519) 877-2901

O.C.I.A.-certified apples and pears, pick-your-own in season, also ready-picked. Apple products, sweet corn and squash in season.

The Big Carrot
348 Danforth Avenue
Toronto, ONT M4K 1N8
(416) 466-2129

Organic produce, bulk and natural foods, vegetarian deli, macrobiotic foods.

The Gentle Rain Natural Food Store
30 Rebecca Street
Stratford, Ont N5A 3P1
(519) 271-0388

Natural and organic foods retailer.

| | |
|---|---|
| The Harvest Wagon<br>1103 Yonge Street<br>Toronto, ONT M4W 2L7<br>(416) 923-7542 | Specialty produce market featuring a wide array of unusual and exotic items from local and global suppliers. Edible flowers, Cookstown greens, organic produce in season. |
| The Peanut Mill<br>191 Welland Avenue,<br>Geneva Square<br>St. Catherines, ONT<br>L2R 2P2<br>(416) 685-8848 | Organic cereals, grains and various natural food products. |
| The Wheat Berry<br>206 rue Main Street<br>Ottawa, ONT K1S 1C6<br>(613) 235-7580 | Organic and natural food store. |
| Windy Lane Farm<br>R.R. #1,<br>6th Concession Road<br>Murillo, ONT P0T 2G0<br>(807) 935-2080 | Kennebeck potatoes; wide variety of garden vegetables and greens. Farm-based retail outlet; suppliers to restaurants and retail stores. |

**QUÉBEC**

| | |
|---|---|
| Aliments Natural Plus<br>955, Jean Gauvin<br>Ste. Foy, PQ G1X 4M5<br>(418) 877-5534 | Organic and health foods, packaged and in bulk. |
| Biojardins Plein Sud<br>Caîsse Postale 325<br>Bassin<br>Îles-de-la-Madeleine,<br>PQ G0B 1A0<br>(418) 937-5388 | Vegetables, herbs, strawberries, tomatoes. |

Dharma
5605, Canterbury
Montréal PQ H3T 1S8
(514) 733-0550

Fresh organic fruits and vegetables.

Ferme Delapointe
R.R. #3, 786, Herringville
Bury, PQ J0R 1J0
(819) 872-3346

Organic cheddar, mild, medium, sharp. Organic maple products.

La Boite à Grains
129, boulevard St. Joseph
Hull, PQ J8Y 3W7
(819) 770-1461

Largest selection of organic product in the Ottawa region. Service in French and English.

L'Essentielle
532, rue de la Madone
Mont Laurier, PQ J9L 1S5
(819) 623-5875

Wide selection of natural and organic foods. Fruits and vegetables.

Le Veau de Charlevoix
76 Ruisseau des Frénes
St. Agnes, PQ G0T 1R0
(418) 439-4258

Producer of grain-fed, free range veal.

Naturosol
1415 des Champs Elysées
Chicoutimi, PQ G7H 6J2
(418) 693-9320

Bulk, unpackaged foods, organic breads, fruits and vegetables, grain-fed chicken.

Sol Épicerie Santé
195 rue Principale
Aylmer, PQ J9H 6J8
(819) 684-0512

Health and natural foods.

## NEW BRUNSWICK

| | |
|---|---|
| Winterwood Natural Foods<br>Box 1665, 51 Broad Street<br>Sussex, N.B. E0E 1P0<br>(506) 433-4195 | Farm eggs, yogurt, butter, certified organic vegetables in season, some from the owner's certified farm, grains and cereals. |

## NOVA SCOTIA

| | |
|---|---|
| Maitland Greenhouses<br>Maitland, N.S. B0N 1T0<br>(902) 261-2109 | Wide variety of organically-grown vegetables and herbs in season. Sale to restaurants and grocery stores. |
| Mary Jane's Alternative Tastes Ltd.<br>1313 Hollis Street<br>Halifax, N.S. B3J 1T8<br>(902) 421-1313 | Largest natural and specialty food store in the Maritimes with certified organic produce all year. |
| Norland Farms<br>R.R. #1<br>Port Williams, N.S.<br>B0P 1T0<br>(902) 542-4655 | Specialists in winter vegetables such as carrots, squash, turnips, leeks, brussels sprouts. Available directly and at the Halifax Farmers' Market. |
| Wild Harvest Products<br>Box 579<br>New Glasgow, N.S.<br>B2H 5E7<br>(902) 755-3222 | Chanterelles in quantity to restaurants and wholesalers in season. |

# Contributors

Ms. Heather Apple
Heritage Seed Program
R.R. #3
Uxbridge, ONT L0C 1K0
(416) 852-7965

Mr. Herb Barbolet
The Glorious Garnish and
Seasonal Salad Co. Ltd.
1374–256th Street
Aldergrove, B.C. V0X 1A0
(604) 857-1400

Ms. Karen Barnaby
The Raintree Restaurant
1630 Alberni Street
Vancouver, B.C. V6G 1A6
(604) 688-5570

Mr. Werner Bassen
Acton's Grill and Café
P.O. Box 39, 268 Main Street
Wolfville, N.S. B0P 1X0
(902) 542-7525

Mr. Neil Baxter
Rundle's Restaurant
9 Cobourg Street
Stratford, ONT N5A 3E4
(519) 271-6442

Mr. Harry Beck
Beck's Bakery
361 Isabella Street
Pembroke, ONT K8A 5T3
(613) 732-2421

M. Yvan Belzile
Le Cabillaud
268 rue Notre-Dame E
Cap-Chat, PQ G0J 1E0
(418) 786-2480

Mr. Paul Boehmer
Opus Restaurant
37 Prince Arthur
Toronto, ONT M5R 1B2
(416) 921-3105

Mr. Christopher Brown
Ecco Il Pane Bakery Inc.
1118 Maple Street
Vancouver, B.C. V6J 3R6
(604) 731-1814

M. Serge Bruyère
À la Table de Serge Bruyère
1200 Rue St. Jean
Québec City, PQ G1R 1S8
(418) 692-2025

Mr. John Christou
Organics Restaurant
568 Parliament Street
Toronto, ONT M4X 1P8
(416) 922-0555

Mr. Brian Clafton
Ramada Renaissance on Bloor
90 Bloor Street East
Toronto, ONT M4W 1A7
(416) 961-8000

Mr. David Cohlmeyer
Cookstown Greens
Box 227
Cookstown, ONT L0L 1L0
(705) 458-9077

M. Domenique Crevoisier
Les Halles
1450 rue Crescent
Montréal, PQ H3G 2B6
(514) 844-2328

Ms. Christina Delano-Stephens
The Alley-Way Café
305 Campbell Stret
Tofino, B.C. V0R 2Z0
(604) 725-3105

Mr. Nigel Didcock
Langdon Hall
R.R. #33
Cambridge, ONT N3H 4R8
(519) 338-8800

Mr. David Feys
Sooke Harbour House
1528 Whiffen Spit Road
R.R. #4
Sooke, B.C. V0S 1N0
(604) 642-3421

Mr. Willy Fida
Angeline's
29 Stanley Street, P.O. Box 16
Bloomfield, ONT K0K 1G0
(613) 393-3301

Mr. Keith Froggett
Scaramouche
1 Benvenuto Place
Toronto, ONT M4V 2L1
(416) 961-8011

Mr. Louis Gervais
Le Meridien
845 Burrard Street
Vancouver, B.C. V6Z 2K6
(604) 682-5511

Mr. Alan Groom
Bacchus Restaurant
Wedgewood Hotel
845 Hornby Street
Vancouver, B.C. V6Z 1V1
(604) 689-7777

Mr. David Heard
The Unheard Of
9602-82 Avenue
Edmonton, AB T6C 0Z7
(403) 432-0480

Mr. Gary Hynes
Cooper's Inn
36 Dock Street
Shelburne, N.S. B0T 1W0
(902) 875-4656

Ms. Dorothy Jackson
The Robin's Nest Bed and Breakfast
Box 2, Site 7
R.R. #8
Calgary, AB T2J 2T9
(403) 931-3514

Mr. Steven James
Cafe Bruges
394 Waterloo Street
London, ONT N6B 2N8
(519) 660-6397

Mr. Jamie Kennedy
Palmerston Restaurant
488 College Street
Toronto, ONT M6G 1A4
(416) 922-9277

Mr. Alain Labrie
Auberge Hatley
P.O. Box 330
North Hatley, PQ J0B 2C0
(819) 842-2451

Ms. Maureen Loucks
The Old Mahle House
Restaurant
2104 Hemer Street
Cedar, B.C. V0R 1J0
(604) 722-3621

Mr. Rick Maddison
Capers
2496 Marine Drive
West Vancouver, B.C.
V6V 1L1
(604) 925-3316

Ms. Lucia Martella
Grano
2035 Yonge Street
Toronto, ONT M4S 2A2
(416) 443-1986

Ms. Ruth McCaslin
Kagiwiosa Manomin Inc.
Box 70
Dinorwic, ONT P0V 1P0
(807) 938-6927

Ms. Alli Millar
Martin's Catering
70 Drewry Avenue
North York, ONT M2M 1C8
(416) 222-6658

Ms. Anne Milne
Monterey Lounge and Grill
Pacific Palisades Hotel
1277 Robson Street
Vancouver, B.C. V6E 1C4
(604) 688-0461

M. Phillippe Mollé
Société Café
1415, rue de la Montagne
Montréal, PQ H3G 1Z3
(514) 987-8168

Ms. Uta Nagel
Grainfields Bakery Ltd.
1464 Kingston Road
Scarborough, ONT M1N 1R6
(416) 691-6061

Ms. Malca Narrol
EastWest
807 Bloor Street W
Toronto, ONT M6G 1L8
(416) 530-1571

Mr. David Nobel
The Unicorn Inn
R.R. #1
South Gillies, ONT P0T 2V0
(807) 475-4200

Mr. Kenneth Peace
O'Keefe Centre
2 Front Street E
Toronto, ONT M5E 1B2
(416) 393-7469

Mr. Sinclair Philip
Sooke Harbour House
1528 Whiffin Spit Road
R.R. #4
Sooke, B.C. V0S 1N0
(604) 642-3421

Mr. Mark Picone
Picone's Food Market
34 King Street
Dundas, ONT L9H 1J7
(416) 628-8642

M. Claude Postel
Claude Postel
443 rue Saint Vincent
Montréal, PQ H2Y 3A6
(514) 875-5067

Mr. Paul Rogalski
La Chaumière
121-17 Avenue SW
Calgary, AB T2G 1H3
(403) 228-5690

Mr. Sheldon Russell
The Church
70 Brunswick Street
Stratford, ONT N5A 3M1
(519) 273-3424

Ms. Lorene Sauro
Cakes and Ayle Ltd.
124 Connie Crescent
Unit 17
Concord, ONT L4K 1L7
(416) 738-3611

Mr. Kevin Snook
The Thirsty Fox
92 Ontario Street S
Grand Bend, ONT N0M 1T0
(519) 238-5181

Mr. Michael Stadtlander
c/o April Point Lodge
P.O. Box 1
Campbell River, B.C.
V9W 4Z9
(604) 285-2222

Mr. Bryan Steele
The Old Prune
151 Albert Street
Stratford, ONT N5A 3K5
(519) 271-5052

Mr. Hubertis Surm
Isadora's Co-op Restaurant
Granville Island
1540 Old Bridge Street
Vancouver, B.C. V6H 3S6
(604) 681-3748

M. Dominique Truchon
Auberge des Peupliers
381, St. Raphael
Cap-à-l'Aigle
Cté Charlevoix, PQ G0T 1B0
(418) 665-4423

Ms. Johanne Vigneault
Restaurant La Table des Roy
C.P. 240-Étang du Nord
Îles de la Madeleine, PQ
G0B 1E0
(418) 986-3004

Mr. Glen van Blommesteim
Overtures
1107 l'Esperance Road
Tecumseh, ONT N8N 1X1
(519) 979-0010

Mr. Wolfgang von Wieser
Four Seasons Hotel
791 West Georgia Street
Vancouver, B.C. V6C 2T4
(604) 689-9333

Mr. Kurt Waldele
Le Café — National Arts Centre
1 Confederation Square
P.O. Box 1534, Stn. "B"
Ottawa, ONT K1P 5W1
(613) 594-5127

Ms. Susan Weaver
Four Seasons Hotel
21 Avenue Road
Toronto, ONT M5R 2G1
(416) 964-0411

# Bibliography


### *Books*

Brown, Lester, *State of the World 1987*, W.W. Norton & Co., 1987.

Creasy, Rosalind, *Cooking from the Garden*, Douglas and McIntyre, Vancouver, 1988

Hardy, Anne, *Where to Eat in Canada*, Oberon Press, 1992

Kennedy, Jamie, *The Jamie Kennedy Cookbook*, Oxford University Press, Toronto, 1985

Kneen, Brewster, *From Land to Mouth*, NC Press Limited, Toronto, 1989

Nimmo, Tomás L., ed., *Directory of Organic Agriculture, 1991–1992*, Canadian Organic Growers, Ottawa, 1991

Robbins, John, *Diet for a New America*, Stillpoint Publishing, Walpole, N.H., 1987

Rodale, J.I. and Staff, *Encyclopedia of Organic Gardening*, Rodale Books Inc., Emmaus, PA., 1975

Waters, Alice, *The Chez Panisse Menu Cookbook*, Random House, N.Y., 1982

### *Speeches and Articles*

Philip, Sinclair, Address to the Stratford Chefs School, March 1992

National Research Council, "Alternative Agriculture," Committee on the Role of Alternative Farming Methods in Modern Production Agriculture, National Academy Press, Washington, D.C., 1989

Organic Crop Improvement Association (Ontario) Inc., "Production and Processing Standards," February 1992

# Index